FAST TRACK TO SUCCESS
STRATEGY

Prentice Hall

FINANCIAL TIMES

In an increasingly competitive world, we believe it's quality of thinking that gives you the edge – an idea that opens new doors, a technique that solves a problem or an insight that simply makes sense of it all. The more you know, the smarter and faster you can go.

That's why we work with the best minds in business and finance to bring cutting-edge thinking and best learning practice to a global market.

Under a range of leading imprints, including *Financial Times Prentice Hall*, we create world-class print publications and electronic products bringing our readers knowledge, skills and understanding, which can be applied whether studying or at work.

To find out more about Pearson Education publications or tell us about the books you'd like to find, you can visit us at **www.pearsoned.co.uk**

FAST TRACK TO SUCCESS

STRATEGY

DAVID McKEAN

FT Prentice Hall
FINANCIAL TIMES

An imprint of **Pearson Education**

Harlow, England • London • New York • Boston • San Francisco • Toronto • Sydney • Singapore • Hong Kong
Tokyo • Seoul • Taipei • New Delhi • Cape Town • Madrid • Mexico City • Amsterdam • Munich • Paris • Milan

PEARSON EDUCATION LIMITED

Edinburgh Gate
Harlow CM20 2JE
Tel: +44 (0)1279 623623
Fax: +44 (0)1279 431059
Website: www.pearsoned.co.uk

First published in Great Britain in 2009

ISBN: 978-0-273-71990-8

British Library Cataloguing-in-Publication Data
A catalogue record for this book is available from the British Library

Library of Congress Cataloging-in-Publication Data
McKean, David, chartered engineer
   Strategy / David McKean.
      p. cm. -- (Fast track to success)
   Includes bibliographical references and index.
   ISBN 978-0-273-71990-8 (pbk. : alk. paper) 1. Strategic planning. 2.
   Management. I. Title.
   HD30.28.M38386 2009
   658.4'012--dc22
                              2009005448

The publisher is grateful for permission to reproduce the following copyright items: Figure on page 48 from 'How competitive forces shape strategy', *Harvard Business Review*, March/April, (Porter, M.E., 1979); Figure on page 66 from 'Strategies of diversification', *Harvard Business Review*, Sept/Oct, (Ansoff, I., 1957).

10 9 8 7 6 5 4 3 2 1
13 12 11 10 09

Series text design by Design Deluxe
Typeset in 10/15 Swis Lt by 30
Printed by Ashford Colour Press Ltd., Gosport

The publisher's policy is to use paper manufactured from sustainable forests.

CONTENTS

THE FAST TRACK WAY

Everything you need to accelerate your career

The best way to fast track your career as a manager is to fast track the contribution you and your team make to your organisation and for your team to be successful in as public a way as possible. That's what the Fast Track series is about. The Fast Track manager delivers against performance expectations, is personally highly effective and efficient, develops the full potential of their team, is recognised as a key opinion leader in the business, and ultimately progresses up the organisation ahead of their peers.

You will benefit from the books in the Fast Track series whether you are an ambitious first-time team leader or a more experienced manager who is keen to develop further over the next few years. You may be a specialist aiming to master every aspect of your chosen discipline or function, or simply be trying to broaden your awareness of other key management disciplines and skills. In either case, you will have the motivation to critically review yourself and your team using the tools and techniques presented in this book, as well as the time to stop, think and act on areas you identify for improvement.

Do you know what you need to know and do to make a real difference to your performance at work, your contribution to your company and your blossoming career? For most of us, the honest answer is 'Not really, no'. It's not surprising then that most of us never reach our full potential. The innovative Fast Track series gives you exactly what you need to speed up your progress and become a high performance manager in all the areas of the business that matter. Fast Track is not just another 'How to' series. Books on selling tell you how to win sales but not how to move from salesperson to sales manager. Project management software enables you to plan detailed tasks but doesn't improve the quality of your project management thinking and business performance. A marketing book tells you about the principles of marketing but not how to lead a team of marketers. It's not enough.

Specially designed features in the Fast Track books will help you to see what you need to know and to develop the skills you need to be successful. They give you:

→ the information required for you to shine in your chosen function or skill – particularly in the Fast Track top ten;

→ practical advice in the form of Quick Tips and answers to FAQs from people who have been there before you and succeeded;

→ state of the art best practice as explained by today's academics and industry experts in specially written Expert Voices;

→ case stories and examples of what works and, perhaps more importantly, what doesn't work;

→ comprehensive tools for accelerating the effectiveness and performance of your team;

→ a framework that helps you to develop your career as well as produce terrific results.

Fast Track is a resource of business thinking, approaches and techniques presented in a variety of ways – in short, a complete performance support environment. It enables managers to build careers from their first tentative steps into management all the way up to becoming a business director – accelerating the performance of their team and their career. When you use the Fast Track approach with your team it provides a common business language and structure, based on best business practice. You will benefit from the book whether or not others in the organisation adopt the same practices; indeed if they don't, it will give you an edge over them. Each Fast Track book blends hard practical advice from expert practitioners with insights and the latest thinking from experts from leading business schools.

The Fast Track approach will be valuable to team leaders and managers from all industry sectors and functional areas. It is for ambitious people who have already acquired some team leadership skills and have realised just how much more there is to know.

If you want to progress further you will be directed towards additional learning and development resources via an interactive Fast Track website, **www.Fast-Track-Me.com**. For many, these books therefore become the first step in a journey of continuous development. So, the Fast Track approach gives you everything you need to accelerate your career, offering you the opportunity to develop your knowledge and skills, improve your team's performance, benefit your organisation's progress towards its aims and light the fuse under your true career potential.

ABOUT THE AUTHOR

DAVID McKEAN is managing director of IT Leaders Ltd, a leading provider of business strategy and technology leadership development. The company has pioneered best-in-class processes in several management disciplines and designed software solutions to support them. He has consulted for many leading clients both in the UK and internationally. Clients include Capita, Barclays, Accenture, the Royal College of Surgeons and BT.

In 1994, David joined Cable & Wireless as the programme director for the third GSM licence in France, securing one of the most profitable licence wins for Cable & Wireless. Since that time, David has worked for several international blue chip companies in Russia, France, Asia and Holland, running large strategy development and business change programmes. In Asia in particular, he worked closely with all parts of the culturally diverse organisation to build a business strategy that would meet the business priorities of the different stakeholders. It was this work that led him to recognise the real difficulties that companies have in understanding a clear process for strategy, providing a rigorous and smart strategy and then having to communicate it to different communities.

David is a regular conference presenter in Europe, the Middle East and Asia on strategy and technology leadership. He is a chartered engineer and a graduate of the University of Cambridge.

David McKean, IT Leaders,
Bix Manor, Henley-on-Thames, Oxfordshire, RG9 4RS, UK
E david.mckean@itleaders.co.uk
T 00 44 (0) 1491 57 86 88

A WORD OF THANKS FROM THE AUTHOR

I would like to thank the following for their generous contributions to this book.

→ **Liz Gooster, Pearson.** There are many exciting new ideas in the publishing world at present, but without an enthusiastic champion, most will simply die a slow death. Liz had the confidence to commission the Fast Track series and associated web-tool on behalf of the Pearson Group at a time when other publishers were cutting back on non-core activities. She has remained committed to its success – providing direction, challenge and encouragement as and when required.

→ **Ken Langdon.** As well as being a leading author in his own right, Ken has worked with all the Fast Track authors to bring a degree of rigour and consistency to the series. As each book has developed, he has been a driving force behind the scenes, pulling the detailed content for each title together in the background – working with an equal measure of enthusiasm and patience!

→ **Mollie Dickenson.** Mollie has a background in publishing and works as a research manager at Henley Business School, and has been a supporter of the project from its inception. She has provided constant encouragement and challenge, and is, as always, an absolute delight to work with.

→ **Critical readers.** As the Fast Track series evolved, it was vital that we received constant challenge and input from other experts and from critical readers.

→ **Professor David Birchall.** David has worked to identify and source Expert Voice contributions from international academic and business experts in each Fast Track title. David is co-author of the Fast Track *Innovation* book and a leading academic author in his own right, and has spent much of the last 20 years heading up the research programme at Henley Business School – one of the world's top ten business schools.

The expert team

Last but not least, I am grateful for the contributions made by experts from around the world in each of the Fast Track titles.

EXPERT	TOPIC	BUSINESS SCHOOL/ COMPANY
Professor Bernard Taylor	Corporate governance – the wake-up call for strategists (p. 18)	Henley Business School, University of Reading and Metacorp Group
Professor Erling S. Andersen	Strategy implementation through projects (p. 30)	Norwegian School of Management, Oslo
Professor David Birchall	The challenges of leadership and strategy making in the third sector (p. 83)	Henley Business School, University of Reading and Metacorp Group
Dr Laurence S. Lyons	Working with your coach (p. 100)	Henley Business School, University of Reading and Metacorp Group
Dr Laurence S. Lyons	Practical strategy (p. 113)	Henley Business School, University of Reading and Metacorp Group
Professor George Tovstiga	Insight-driven strategy – scoping the boundary conditions (p. 134)	Henley Business School, University of Reading and Metacorp Group
Dr Jean-Anne Stewart	Making it happen – the facilitation bit (p. 154)	Henley Business School, University of Reading and Metacorp Group
Dr Rebecca Steliaros	Where does innovation fit into strategy? (p. 169)	Engineering and Physical Sciences Research Council, Swindon

STRATEGY FAST TRACK

This book is for both strategy generalists and specialists, in fact for anyone who wants and expects to develop strategy. Most managers will be involved in creating strategy at some point in their career and, typically, the more senior they become, the more time they will spend on formulating plans for the future. It is, of course, considered the most important activity of the chief executive officer. It seems logical to assume, therefore, that the better you are at it, the more likely you are to reach the top job. Even though strategy may only be part of your job responsibility, your success in this area will tell everyone a lot about your capabilities and potential.

Much has been written about different strategy techniques and it is not my objective to explain all the models that exist today. That said, for a manager to move up the strategy ladder, they will need a background in some of the more common techniques, not least to carry on a sensible conversation with those who are well versed in strategic theory. This book will give you an introduction to many of the more common or better known techniques, as well as references to find out further information. Be careful not to overdose on the theory – too much of it stops you from spending time on the more valuable activities of strategy, namely good networking, crisp planning and effective implementation. There are many good approaches to developing strategy. The sooner you find one that works, the better it will be for you, your business and your career.

This book approaches strategy from the practical standpoint of someone working in a real organisation. It shows how they can enhance their contribution through three stages of development.

1 Building an understanding of what the strategy is.

2 Contributing to the development of strategy.

3 Leading the process to create a strategic plan.

Each of these three stages requires a deeper knowledge of how to create a strategic plan. There is no right or wrong way to do this, no rules or regulations to say what must be done or the order things should be done in. Nonetheless, it does make sense to have a guiding structure or process to follow. To this end, I have described ten clear steps for making a strategic plan. The process includes much of the recent and established thinking on strategy, allowing you to make good progress without spending too much time on the theory. When you've read the ten steps, you will realise that you don't need to do every part in detail. For example, when creating the high-level plan, you must have a set of objectives, but you don't necessarily need a 'statement of beliefs'. By the end, you will also be able to relate these ten steps to the strategy in your organisation. This will help you understand it better and identify possible areas for improvement.

It is also possible to do things in a different order. For example, some companies start with the high-level aspects of a plan. Some start at the more granular level. One of my clients recently described a 'bouncing ball' approach, where they started at the high level, worked through to the lower levels and then summarised back to the top level. This took some time the first time they did it, but it meant the whole company bought into the strategy – and they got faster each year. Remember, there is no right or wrong answer. The most important thing is to develop a method that suits you and your situation.

So, at a high level, what are we trying to achieve? As the figure below shows, you need to know your starting point (point A) and your destination (point B). Your destination will be shaped by the forces of opportunities and threats (C) along the way. The work you have to do in your strategic plan (D) is then simply B minus A. In terms of the order you do things in, it

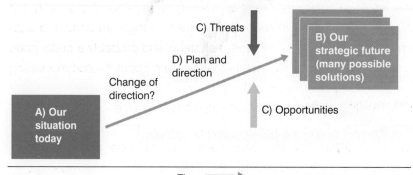

doesn't really matter – some start with the destination (B) and some with the starting point (A), but you need both to complete your plan.

Make each step simple and practical, but look to improve the process year on year, bit by bit, rather than trying to get it perfect first time. Keep things moving and stick to your target milestones, or you'll spend for ever doing analysis, rather than producing something useful. One group I worked with a few years ago had spent a lot of time setting the high-level objectives and crafting their mission, vision and value statements, but they failed to translate this into meaningful steps of what actually needed to be done. This overanalysis stopped them getting the real benefit of a good strategy. It is a bit like New Year's resolutions. Agreeing the high-level goal is not sufficient – you need a set of specific actions to actually make it happen.

Of course, most companies do manage to create an action list or, more realistically, a project list. Unfortunately, not many take a step back and ask the two crucial questions. Firstly, 'Will this really help me achieve what I want?' and secondly, 'Is there a better way?' In other words, they come up with an initial strategy and forget to look at other options. These 'strategic choices' are essential to optimise results, mitigate strategic risk and create resilience to the pitfalls of business change.

In the real world, the puzzle of strategy is usually shared between different groups, each one with its own part to play in the overall plan. Most executives start at this level, typically helping their manager by contributing to one particular aspect of strategy. For an executive to be successful in their career, it is vital that they get involved in this as soon as possible. They will then learn how the whole plan fits together and how each part of the organisation supports the other. Goals can then be linked easily with the individual objectives of all team members and should become a part of their performance reviews. If all of these things are done in a well-organised manner, you will have a strategy, and probably a pretty good one at that. Now you can start telling everyone about it – communicating the plan is a crucial step in realising the value of strategy.

Many organisations regard strategic planning as a 'once a year thing' and operate for a lot of the year with a strategy that becomes more and more out of date. This can make them unresponsive to market changes. A sudden change in economic conditions (e.g. a US housing crisis) or government regulation (e.g. Home Information Packs in the UK housing market) are just a couple of examples of market changes that may require you to quickly review your strategy. At the same time, you need to keep monitoring your competitors; they're not going to stand still for a year and their activities can invalidate all or part of the sales and marketing strategy. To solve this, you need a method of reviewing your strategy and changing it when and where needed. You have to check continually that the projects you're doing still fall within the strategy.

Setting strategy is not a completely collaborative process and not everyone gets a chance to vote. All the more reason, therefore, to look out for opportunities to get involved. The first step in this is to show that you are interested in the company and its future. Start by asking questions about why certain things are the way they are. There is, of course, a right and a wrong way to ask these questions, so be sensitive. Nonetheless, if it is done properly, you will start to challenge the status quo and this will enhance your profile. If you can translate what you learn into opportunities, your chances of playing a key role in the development of strategy will be enhanced.

It is probable that you already have some experience with strategy. That experience is unique to you and has come from your own knowledge, work and success. This book uses a coaching style and, as with any coach, you may find that some of the advice rings true and some is less relevant. Knowing what you know and therefore adding to what you have learnt is essential. Getting to the top in strategy is a never-ending quest, so keep building on that experience rather than reinventing the wheel. For example, if you want to do risk analysis you'll find a method in the book, but if you have another one that you prefer, then you should go on using that. You will no doubt have some tools and techniques that are useful in developing strategy that you want to continue using. Think about where they fit in the ten-step strategy process and use them appropriately. A lot of the steps are relevant and similar for most companies, but there are differences and they can be important. Remember, it is your knowledge and experience that sets you apart.

When you have cracked the concepts of strategy and learnt how to implement them successfully, the sky is the limit – you're on your way to being a director of a major organisation. Good strategic thinking and planning give a career a terrific boost. If you really want to get to the top, you will want to get there fast, so let's get on the fast track.

HOW TO USE THIS BOOK

Fast Track books present a collection of the latest tools, techniques and advice to help build your team and your career. Use this table to plan your route through the book.

PART	OVERVIEW
About the author	A brief overview of the author, his background and his contact details
A **Awareness**	*This first part gives you an opportunity to gain a quick overview of strategy and to reflect on your current effectiveness*
1 *Strategy in a nutshell*	A brief overview of strategy and a series of frequently asked questions to bring you up to speed quickly
2 *Strategy audit*	Simple checklists to help identify strengths and weaknesses in your team and your capabilities
B **Business Fast Track**	*Part B provides tools and techniques that may form part of the strategy framework for you and your team*
3 *Fast Track top ten*	Ten tools and techniques used to help you implement a sustainable approach to strategy based on the latest best practice
4 *Technologies*	A review of the latest information technologies used to improve effectiveness and efficiency of strategy activities
5 *Implementing change*	A detailed checklist to identify gaps and to plan the changes necessary to implement your strategy framework
C **Career Fast Track**	*Part C focuses on you, your leadership qualities and what it takes to get to the top*
6 *The first ten weeks*	Recommended activities when starting a new role in strategy, together with a checklist of useful facts to know
7 *Leading the team*	Managing change, building your team and deciding your leadership style
8 *Getting to the top*	Becoming a strategy professional, getting promoted and becoming a director – what does it take?
D **Director's toolkit**	*The final part provides more advanced tools and techniques based on industry best practice*
Toolkit	Advanced tools and techniques used by senior managers
Glossary	Glossary of terms

FAST-TRACK-ME.COM

Throughout this book you will be encouraged to make use of the companion site: **www.Fast-Track-Me.com**. This is a custom-designed, highly interactive online resource that addresses the needs of the busy manager by providing access to ideas and methods that will improve individual and team performance quickly. Top features include:

→ **Health Checks.** Self-audit checklists allowing evaluation of you and your team against industry criteria. You will be able to identify areas of concern and plan for their resolution using a personal 'Get-2-Green' action plan.

→ **The Knowledge Cube.** The K-Cube is a two-dimensional matrix presenting Fast Track features from all topics in a consistent and easy-to-use way – providing ideas, tools and techniques in a single place, anytime, anywhere. This is a great way to delve in and out of business topics quickly.

→ **The Online Coach.** The Online Coach is a toolkit of fully interactive business templates in MS Word format that allow Fast-Track-Me.com users to explore specific business methods (strategy, ideas, projects etc.) and learn from concepts, case examples and other resources according to your preferred learning style.

→ **Business Glossary.** The Fast Track Business Glossary provides a comprehensive list of key words associated with each title in the Fast Track series, together with a plain English definition – helping you to cut through business jargon.

The website can also help answer some of the vital questions managers are asking themselves today (see figure overleaf).

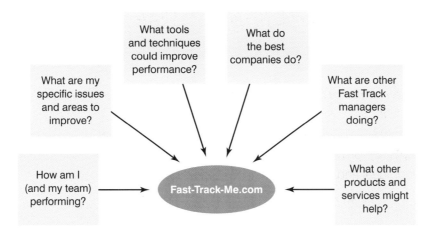

Don't get left behind: log on to **www.Fast-Track-Me.com** now to get your career on the fast track.

AWARENESS

This book introduces a sustainable approach to developing your involvement in strategy planning, aimed at keeping you, your team and your organisation at the forefront of strategic thinking, thus contributing towards the future of all three. The starting point is to gain a quick understanding of what strategy is and what it is not, and to understand your own and your team's capabilities today. For this reason I will ask you a number of questions that will reveal the role that strategy plays in your activities and those of the team around you. The questions look at the plans you currently have in place, how well you work with others to keep your strategy current and your flexibility in changing business conditions.

It is important that you do an open and honest self-audit as you set up your framework for developing strategy. The stakes are high. Strategy is at the heart of success in this global, competitive marketplace. You will need to show strong leadership skills and motivate your team to look to the future. Poor leadership and poor team effectiveness will make failure likely. An effective team poorly led will sap the team's energy and lead in the long term to failure, as team members become demotivated or, worse still, leave the organisation. Leading an ineffective team can still deliver results, but it will be difficult. So, looking at the figure below, how do you make sure that you and your team are in the top right-hand box – an effective team with an excellent leader? That's what this book is about, and this section will help you discover your starting point.

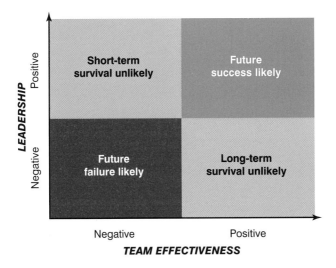

STRATEGY IN A NUTSHELL

Starting with the basics

Just what is strategy?

The word 'strategy' can be very confusing. Different people use it to mean slightly different things. It can mean a major activity, as in 'one of our strategies is to implement a new CRM system'. Sometimes it is used to express a future outcome, such as 'our strategy is to move into the business-to-business market'. I even hear some managers use it to mean 'very important' as in 'I am working on a strategic project for the chairman'.

The word comes from the Greek *strategos* (plural *strategoi*; Greek στρατηγός) meaning 'army leader' or 'general'. The derivation of the word helps us to understand the modern dictionary definition as follows:

Strategy (n) – A plan to achieve a long-term aim.

Whilst this is accurate at a high level, the following definition is more helpful for our purposes:

⋅ **Strategy** – Defining the best future for your team or organisation, mapping the route to achieve it and communicating it clearly.

There are four important aspects to this definition.

 1 Strategy strives to define the best future, not just the most obvious or an extrapolation of the past.

2 It has to be achievable.

3 There needs to be a logical route to achieve it.

4 Finally, it must be communicated clearly to the organisation for it to become reality.

Why is it so important?

As the Greek definition suggests, strategy (sometimes called the 'art of the general') is not a new concept. It was a crucial part of winning battles, where it was not enough to have large numbers of courageous and well-trained soldiers. They needed to be fighting battles that they could win. Strategy in business is no different.

The markets of today are similar to the battlefields of yesterday. The products and services are the weapons. Strategy is about finding the best products and services to compete in the right markets at the right time. Those that understand strategy, and in my experience they are very few, are on a fast track to success in business.

Strategy as a key business skill really is more important now than ever before. Most large companies put together a list of the skills or characteristics, called competency lists, which they look for in their executives, managers and senior leaders. The ability to think strategically always appears near the top. This is not just coincidence – there are some very specific changes in business that have led to this. Here are three examples of trends which serve to demonstrate the increase in the importance of strategy to survival.

❦ 1 The working environment

Not that long ago, the majority of employees would receive almost all their information about the future of the company from their immediate bosses. As each manager communicated to their team, they would modify the message, perhaps leaving out some higher-level details, until, by the time the message reached the sharp end of the business, it had been diffused, sometimes out of all recognition. Different parts of the business would inevitably hear different messages and they would in turn strive for slightly different goals. In the business world of today, key messages from the senior management are communicated immediately to the rest of the organisation through emails, webcasts or the intranet. The ability of companies to unite behind one clear set of objectives and a vision of the future is stronger than it has ever been.

● Technology has transformed the way that people within an organisation do their work. Many of the managers I work with are driven by the sheer volume of email that they need to handle; reading, assessing and responding to messages as well as reviewing countless large documents. Their speed of doing business is so much faster than 30 or 40 years ago. Unfortunately, if you are travelling faster, but along the wrong road, you can get very lost, very quickly. Again, a clear and uniting strategy – a roadmap, to use the analogy – is more important than ever.

● Technology has also made it easier for teams to work in different locations. Many employees now have the option to work from home, using broadband to connect to office software applications. Companies communicate with their customers and suppliers as if they were members of the same team. This is much more efficient and has the additional benefits of flexibility, the ability to work free from distractions (perhaps not always, particularly if you have small children!) and some cost savings. However, having employees spread over such a large area makes it more important for the senior management to communicate clear and consistent goals to the workforce – one of the primary roles of good strategy.

2 Globalisation

No matter how big or small you are, you are competing in a global market. The corner shop, struggling with higher prices because it lacks the buying muscle of the big boys, is now also competing head to head with sellers on eBay, and with a national retailer offering home delivery. Increasing competition from the BRICK countries (Brazil, Russia, India, China and Korea) effectively means that Western companies can no longer compete on the basis of price. Stock market changes in one country can have a significant effect on the financial stability of another, not in a matter of months as it used to be, but in a matter of hours. Particularly in Europe, companies are merging and the workforce is becoming increasingly international. According to *Forbes* magazine, 33 per cent of UK CEOs are non-British citizens, 10 per cent of US CEOs are non-US citizens and 33 per cent of US CEOs have had some international experience. Strategic planning now has to take into account a much greater scope of possibilities. It must consider both threats and opportunities from all around the world and be more responsive.

The good news is that we have more opportunities to go after and we can achieve levels of success never before thought possible. On the other hand, if we restrict our thinking, we can find our competitive success drifting away at an alarming rate. Having a crisp, efficient process for developing strategy that allows us to review and react quickly has become an essential part of doing business.

3 Product life cycle times

How many of us have bought some item of technology – a new computer, mobile phone or television, for example – only to go back to the shop a month later and see a newer model on the shelves, often for a lower price? This rate of progress in improving service and reducing costs has led to changes in how organisations go about their tasks, and this often means major changes in the way work is organised.

There are two important issues. The first is how well you produce the products and services that your customers want today. The second is how well you will meet the needs of those customers in the future. The first requires operational efficiency, the second requires strategic planning.

There is a helpful analogy for the difference between an efficient organisation and one that has a clear strategy. A company with an efficient operation and no strategy would make the best black and white televisions in the world. A company with a clear strategy and poor operations might have a great design for a new flat-screen technology but no ability to make it. Clearly to be a successful manufacturer of televisions you need good operations and good strategy.

 CASE STORY *TRAINING SERVICES, JEN'S STORY*

Narrator Jen was the training director for a US computer training company, with responsibility for implementing strategy.

Context During a period of fast growth, a US-based computer training company was adding new courses to its training course portfolio. The company was being asked whether it could deliver management training courses as well as the computer courses. Course quality was falling as the instructors were not familiar with the specialist skills required to deliver such courses.

Issue Although the published strategy gave guidelines about which courses were available to be sold, the sales director kept ignoring it and simply bullied the training people into meeting the customers' needs. The falling course quality was starting to jeopardise the company's reputation.

Solution Jen was the training director responsible for course delivery. She brought the issue to the attention of the senior management team. As a result, they asked her to sign off on all training proposals to ensure they aligned with the strategy guidelines. Where new courses were being proposed, the sales director had to commit to covering all new design and trainer costs in the proposal.

Learning Strategy is important to provide guidance for a company and control its future growth, but it must be adhered to. For fast-growing companies, it is important not to let the long-term strategy be diverted by a short-term opportunity.

This shorter product life cycle and the pressures it brings can mean turbulent times for employees who find it ever more difficult to maintain their loyalty to one company. Strategy has an important role to play in guiding employees through these difficult times. It provides a set of cultural values that reassures staff, builds loyalty and, of course, ultimately helps retain high-quality people. And that makes good business sense.

So why is it so difficult – what typically goes wrong?

As well as helping organisations to develop their strategy, I have run many seminars with business colleagues on how to do it. We start the seminar by asking delegates what typically goes wrong with setting strategy. Although all the delegates understand the importance of developing strategy, it is surprising how many things stand in the way of a successful outcome. As you read the examples below, think about which apply to your organisation and how you would avoid or counter these potential problems in your own situation.

1 **Strategy is considered highly confidential.** Some organisations believe that it is solely the responsibility of the board of directors to develop strategy. Strategic planning only takes place at the board meetings and the results are kept

confidential. Whilst the board of directors clearly has the most important role to play in strategy, it is also important that the rest of the organisation understands and contributes to the future direction. Of course discretion is still advisable in some cases; for example, if competitors have advance knowledge about a strategic acquisition initiative it might jeopardise a successful outcome. Strategic responsibility needs to be joined up across all levels of an organisation.

2 **The company finds it difficult to move on from past successes.** When a company has been successful for a long time, it can be difficult to see why it will not continue into the future. Companies get into the habit of mistaking long-term planning for strategy. Their future is defined by projecting financial results from the past. These companies develop something of a 'blind spot' as to the invincibility of their products, usually brought about by a lack of product testing or review by outsiders. Sooner or later a new market entrant or a disruptive technology transforms the market, leaving the company unprepared and unable to respond.

3 **There is no structure or method.** This lowers the probability of success. Often the people who are responsible for strategy have used different methods in the past. This can cause a misalignment in how strategy should be developed, which can be very time consuming. There needs to be a clear purpose and a structured process. Furthermore, using the same method for successive years means that proper assessments can be made of what worked and what didn't. Adjustments can be made to improve both the process and the output. I find that the companies most successful at creating strategy have developed their own process over several years.

4 **Not enough time is allowed or it takes too long.** All too often people are too busy with day-to-day operations to stop and think, let alone plan the future. As individuals, we may be too reactive – responding to one email crisis or another. At the other extreme, strategy can be made too difficult, requiring senior management to be tied up full-time for days. This damages the

day-to-day operation, and often the outputs from such assessments are too detailed to withstand the test of time. The right balance needs to be struck. Strategic planning needs to be kept apart from operational issues and carefully planned so it does not overly disrupt day-to-day activities.

5 **Strategy tries to do everything.** Some companies treat strategy like they would New Year's resolutions, promising to be successful in areas that they had not been in the past. It becomes an additional list of things to do. An important aspect of strategy is not just what you do, but also what you don't do. Organisations talk about focusing on many different things but, by definition, focus can only be applied to a small number of priorities.

6 **The strategy is not joined up.** One of the most common problems is where the strategy 'does not add up'. A strategy is developed requiring new products and new markets but without the necessary people, systems or budget. For a strategy to be successful it needs to be integrated. The capabilities such as marketing support, human resources and information technology need to work together with the necessary funding to support each other in achieving one coherent goal.

7 **Strategy is kept high-level and has no supporting plan of activities.** Strategy has to paint a high-level picture, but if it is not grounded in practice, it risks being unachievable or inappropriate. It also needs to create a sense of urgency and act as the catalyst to kick off the key projects. Practical considerations mean that these initiatives should be done in order of priority. A clear plan will also tell the organisation what is expected of individuals so that they can support it. This is an important step because it demonstrates that strategy is not a paper exercise, which in turn helps to get buy-in.

8 **Strategy is not communicated.** The best strategy in the world will count for nothing if it is not well communicated. Different types of communication are required for different audiences. Board presentations might require details of financial growth and investment. Presentations to a wider audience might focus

more on telling stories that illustrate what success looks like in terms that people can relate to.

9 **Strategy is not flexible.** Strategy needs to be flexible and agile to take advantage of new opportunities and threats. Reviewing strategy just once a year can often be insufficient, as market forces change quickly. Regular reviews of strategy are more effective than a large planning exercise once a year.

10 **No one knows when it has been successful.** Measuring the success of strategy is very important. Metrics should mean something to those who are responsible for delivering results. So, for example, if an objective is to increase market share by 10 per cent, it needs to be clear what this means for the company itself. If the company increased earnings and profit by 20 per cent, but so did the competition, does this count as a success, even though market share didn't increase? Careful consideration needs to be given when specifying metrics and clearly understanding their impact on behaviour.

These potential pitfalls can be addressed in isolation, or as part of an integrated framework as presented in Chapter 3. It may be worth taking a minute to think about which of these obstacles you have come across in your career. Are there additional reasons that have not been mentioned here? It is often worth making a note of them so they can be addressed. Successful strategic planning is all about continuing to do things better.

QUICK TIP LEARNING FROM THE PAST
Think about the last time you were involved in developing strategic plans. Which aspects of the plan were successful and which weren't?

So just what is strategy? – frequently asked questions

The following table provides quick answers to some of the most frequently asked questions about strategy. Use this as a way of gaining a quick overview.

FAQ 1 What is strategy?	1 In its simplest form, strategy is merely the creation of a high-level plan with information on how to achieve its goals. However, in the context of business, strategy is better defined as a long-term, achievable plan that will provide competitive advantage for a company in the future, based on predicted trends and customer buying habits.
FAQ 2 Why is strategy important to our business when profits and revenues are good?	2 Strategy ensures the future of an organisation. There are many examples of companies who were successful over a long period of time but whose businesses failed because of a reluctance to plan long term, or recognise and accept that markets were changing. Many companies lost substantial market share by being slow to adopt the internet; conversely, many internet companies failed because their strategy overestimated their achievable market share. IBM is a good example of a company that was slow to adjust its strategy away from proprietary hardware solutions, and it took several years during the 1990s to re-establish itself as a strong technology force, particularly in the area of web solutions.
FAQ 3 Who should be involved in the strategy process?	3 Strategy often starts at the top level with the board of directors, but it is an iterative process and should involve leaders and managers from the whole organisation, with employees and business partners having the opportunity to provide new ideas. Strategic responsibility exists at all levels – it is essential that you are involved in that process. If you have people working for you, assign some of them to help. Avoid having too many people involved in the writing of the deliverables, as your strategy runs the risk of becoming too labour intensive, too detailed or merely extrapolating past performance into the future.
FAQ 4 How coordinated should strategy activities be – does this not suppress flexibility?	4 Many organisations make the mistake of creating strategy without a plan of key activities and milestones. The best strategies have to be achievable and, realistically, this will only happen with a high-level plan of activities. The communication of the strategic plan or roadmap really helps employees to visualise the work ahead and makes a successful outcome more likely. One way to get involved in strategy is to offer to create this common plan. It will give you a great opportunity to meet with the other key players in the strategy process.
FAQ 5 What is the best way to build strategy?	5 There is no single best way to build strategy. Different companies follow different processes

and use different frameworks. The important thing is that the entire organisation follows the same process so that the outputs are consistent and the strategy is coherent and aligned. Find out what process is in place where you work and compare it with the model in this book.

FAQ 6 *How do you know if you have chosen the right strategy?*

6   Unfortunately you won't – strategy is an ongoing process and there is no single right answer. The best you can do is to use key performance metrics to measure results. Tracking these is the only way to assess if the strategy is working. Make sure you document the baseline assumptions that went into your plan so you can validate them subsequently. Of course, you will never know for sure if an alternative strategy would have got you a better result. What is more important is that you learn from the past but keep looking to the future.

FAQ 7 *How does strategy link to long-term success?*

7   Continuously improving what you are doing today may not be enough for long-term survival let alone success. If your industry is changing rapidly, then only improving dramatically on an existing product or breaking into a new market can set you apart from competitors. It is the job of strategy to think through what these changes might be and provide more assurance for success in the future.

FAQ 8 *How often should we review our strategy?*

8   The strategy review period will often depend on the organisation itself. In the mobile telephone market, for example, the product life cycle is four months. In contrast, a power station may have a working life of 20 years, and clearly the review period with regard to its output capability (but not its pricing strategy!) will be much less frequent.

FAQ 9 *How can we make strategy visible across the business?*

9   Of those companies that have developed a clear strategy, the single most important area that differentiates them is in the area of communication. Once the strategy has been completed, it is important that a communications plan is put together. This should include 'town hall' meetings where the senior management explains the key themes to the whole organisation. These sessions should be interesting and have an opportunity for informal discussion afterwards. Too many presentation slides can alienate a large audience and miss the opportunity to make the employees feel part of the future. More detail can be made available through the company's website, email and team meetings. Research also shows that organisations that tailor their strategic messages

to different audiences are more successful. Communicating strategy is important for a second reason – it provides an early feedback mechanism to respond to changes. Think about your own role in strategy. How did you hear about the company strategy? How do think it could be improved? In relation to your own work on strategy, how do you currently communicate it to your peers and work colleagues?

FAQ 10 How much budget should be allocated to strategic initiatives?

10 All of a company's activities should be linked in some way to its strategy, including the allocation of financial resources. Even though top-level strategy should identify the main programme initiatives, it is still important that each of these programmes is properly analysed in terms of the human and financial resources required. In their enthusiasm to develop a new strategy, organisations sometimes identify too many programmes. These can add an unsustainable burden on the organisation in terms of activity levels and the financial investment required.

FAQ 11 What is the best way of filtering out bad strategic ideas?

11 This is a common problem in developing strategy, as the correct answer will only be known at some time in the future. Some organisations start their strategic process with the view that no idea is a bad idea. The problem often lies in the fact that people tend to have an emotional attachment to their own ideas and it can be difficult to exclude them diplomatically. One technique that can help is Edward de Bono's six hat method.[1] In this, participants are asked to look at all ideas in turn, first evaluating the advantages and then the disadvantages. This rational evaluation technique helps ideas to be excluded in an objective way.

FAQ 12 How can we encourage our organisation to think of new approaches?

12 The 'first idea we thought of' strategy is one that I see very frequently in strategic discussions. Senior managers start out by believing that only incremental improvements are needed. While this may be true in stable environments, good strategic thinkers should always be looking at other options. One effective approach is to look at different strategic scenarios in the future. By comparing the different outcomes, it is often easier to assess which combination of activities is likely to deliver the better strategy. An alternative method is to have one of the creative participants go away and imagine they were creating the strategy for one of the competitors. This can often create a sense of urgency that was previously missing.

[1] de Bono, Edward (1986) *Six Thinking Hats*, Harmondsworth: Viking

FAQ 13 Should we involve our customers in developing strategy?	13	Absolutely! Your existing customers will know a lot about how your products work and will have many suggestions for how to make them better. Many organisations have focus groups which regularly review their performance. However, to get a broad perspective, you will need to include other sources, not least companies or consumers who use competitive products. You may also want to involve your key suppliers.
FAQ 14 How long should it take to develop a new strategy?	14	Although business strategy normally takes a three- or five-year view, most organisations review their plans in detail every year. On average, each full review takes two or three months, with the first month being an analysis of the current situation before the teams get together to discuss ways forward. If you try to do it significantly quicker (say in less than a month), you risk not having enough information to make decisions, and if you take substantially more time, you can have an adverse effect on the day-to-day operations. It is important that you choose what is right for you and your organisation. If you have just started a new job, you should look to get involved with strategic planning as soon as possible – even if a 'new version' has just been published.
FAQ 15 Are strategic planners born or made?	15	It is true that some people are naturally better at strategic planning than others. But it is a myth to think that these people are like chess grand masters who have considered every option and a corresponding counter move. The reality is that developing effective strategy needs many individual skills, including the analysis of data, big-picture thinking, creativity, innovation and team leadership to name just a few. It is rare that one person excels in all these areas, and I have consistently found that the most effective strategic planning is done by close-working groups, usually with complementary skills. Try to get involved in all stages, including data analysis, brainstorming, planning and communication. The greater your experience, the better you will be.
FAQ 16 What is the link between strategy and long-term planning?	16	Long-term planning is the process that companies use to predict what future resources might be required if the business continues to perform as it currently does, with a steady year-on-year growth. It usually defines the future in terms of sales forecasts and the corresponding financial projections including revenue and profit. Because of the compounded projections, it also tends to overestimate performance, since it usually assumes little growth in product scope or markets.

Strategy should be considered as a separate process, where the products and markets of a company are considered based on an independent assessment of the future market conditions. This approach takes into account all environmental factors, including advances in technology, legislative, competitive and social change. Strategy therefore does not necessarily include all the detailed financial forecasts, instead focusing more on business priorities and direction.

FAQ 17 *How radically should our new strategy change the business?*	**17**	The answer of course depends on your particular business and how successful it is. In general, the more successful the company, the less it should look to overhaul what it is doing. In his book, *From Good to Great*, Jim Collins[2] found that those companies who maintained extraordinary success had identified what they could do better than anyone else in the world and kept their focus on this. However, even the highly successful companies should never be complacent and should always be looking for fast-moving market trends and the changing needs of customers. In contrast, a company that is experiencing a downturn in its success needs to look more carefully at the root of this and should be more willing to consider radical changes to its business, in terms of the products it offers, the markets it serves and the effectiveness of its internal operations.
FAQ 18 *Will developing new strategy prevent us from addressing operational priorities?*	**18**	The short answer is yes – if you let it. A number of clients have told me that the secret to minimising the impact and time spent on strategy is to ensure that everyone understands the process, what they need to do as individuals, and then commits to meeting the project timelines as a group. It is recommended, therefore, that operations and strategy are discussed separately. This allows operational decisions to be made without long discussions on strategy. Conversely, strategy needs to be discussed without being constantly interrupted by urgent (and not necessarily important) problems. One issue that I see more and more is the curse of mobile email devices. If you are about to chair a discussion on strategy, ask everyone to turn them off and don't start until they have. If the building catches fire, you will hopefully smell the smoke or hear the fire alarm first!

[2]Collins, Jim (2001), *Good to Great*, New York: HarperBusiness.

FAQ 19 *How do you prevent corporate politics from getting in the way of developing good strategy?*	**19** Like it or not, corporate politics exists to a greater or lesser extent in all organisations. Corporate politics is usually about power and often about a resistance to change. Since strategy is about identifying how the company must change, it is no surprise that politics is often present. There is no simple answer, but whatever the situation, a good strategist recognises that solving political problems is about understanding people, their motivations and spheres of influence. You will then be able to incorporate them in a positive way into the new strategic plans, without compromising the end result.
FAQ 20 *What happens if we get it wrong?*	**20** It depends how wrong you have got it! Good strategy will have contingencies that mitigate problems as they arise. Most often, strategies fail to deliver in one area or do not deliver results as quickly as hoped. If this is the case, it is important to have regular reviews of strategy. Generally these will be to discuss smaller-scale changes to the plans to bring them back on target.

I hope that these FAQs give a quick start to getting to grips with strategy. The rest of this book shows you how to move from understanding what the key elements of strategy are to an active implementation of strategy either within your team or division, or company-wide.

QUICK TIP MARKET INFORMATION

Get into the habit of building up market information during the year in a structured way so the background information you need is available at the beginning of the strategic planning process.

Corporate governance – the wake-up call for strategists

Professor Bernard Taylor

EXPERT VOICE

A number of company failures in the last ten years which were the result of corporate mismanagement (Enron and Worldcom being the most notable) led to a serious decline in trust. Whilst it may well have just been that a 'few bad apples' were found out, it has resulted in a questioning of the effectiveness of corporate governance. This has been further questioned during the 2007/08 banking crisis, starting in the UK with Northern Rock.

The American investor Warren Buffet once said, 'It's only when the tide goes out that you get to see who's been swimming with their trunks off'. Following the scandals in 2001/02 in the US, many of the players in the Western corporate governance system were found wanting. This has been further exacerbated in the eyes of the public by the fact that CEOs in 23 firms investigated in the US took home $1.4bn in remuneration between 1999 and 2001 whilst at the same time laying off 16,200 employees and presiding over a loss of share value of $530bn, about 73 per cent of their market value. In addition, investment banks were accused of promoting the shares of companies which they knew were having problems. Arthur Andersen partners were found guilty of shredding documents relating to Enron, for whom they were the auditors.

Steps have since been taken to reduce the likelihood of such scandals occurring again. In the UK, the Combined Code of Practice in Corporate Governance and, in the US, the Sarbanes-Oxley Act have been implemented. The latter applies not only to transactions within the US but also for any company with a US listing. In consequence, the impact could be far-reaching. The penalties for misbehaviour are high – significant fines and jail sentences of up to 20 years.

But what led to the 2001/02 crisis? There are three key factors: the dot.com bubble and the stock market crash; high-risk strategies; and insider greed.

The rapid development of the internet created new opportunities for businesses and consumers. Equipment and software providers, internet server and content suppliers responded. However, the early claims were grossly exaggerated. Share prices, having risen dramatically on 9 March 2001, fell catastrophically. This was further exacerbated by the US corporate scandals resulting from poor governance. The shareholders who suffered included many individuals encouraged to join what Margaret Thatcher had termed 'the share-owning democracy'. By the end of 2000 more than 40 million Americans had about $1.7 trillion invested largely in mutual funds. Also in the US direct investment in shares expanded to as many as 85 million people – it became known as an 'equity culture'. The investment advice they received was often of questionable value. In the UK confidence in the life insurance industry was undermined by scandals such as the mis-selling of personal pensions. The problems were not confined to the US and UK. Ahold, a Dutch company, acquired 50 companies in the 1990s and earnings soared 15 per cent per annum. But in 2003 the executive admitted overstating the company's earnings in the US and Argentina by at least $500m. The shares fell nearly 90 per cent from their peak. Irregular accounting practices have been unearthed. Another factor is the extent to which boards of directors allowed chief executives to pursue very risky strategies. For example, the rush by companies such as Vivendi Universal and AOLTimeWarner to merge was based on anticipated synergies between media and the internet which then didn't materialise. As a result, billions of dollars in shareholder value were destroyed. Also, many bank mergers failed to deliver the benefits which had been sold to shareholders as justification. One notable example in the UK is Marconi, which over-extended itself by a risky strategy only to fail spectacularly.

But not all shareholders have lost out. Many company executives benefited from inflated salaries; many investment bankers, lawyers, accountants and auditors were also winners.

One may ask if we have learnt the lessons from these earlier scandals and whether steps taken by regulatory bodies have been sufficient. Certainly recent world events would raise doubts, and governments are now rethinking the regulation of banks, but this rethink will no doubt extend beyond this one sector to embrace the governance of all enterprises towards their stakeholders.

A number of changes in behaviour are essential to restore public confidence. All parties in the 'corporate reporting supply chain' (management, the board, accountants, auditors, investment bankers and analysts, information providers, standards setters, regulators, institutional investors and fund managers, individual investors and pensioners) need to accept that they are accountable to the shareholders and they must provide full and honest reports.

After Enron, Marconi and the dotcom bubble many boards were reformed and made more independent of management. However, in 2007/08 the credit crunch has revealed that boards need to play a more active role, particularly in risk management, controlling executive pay and 'the bonus culture'.

Those working on strategy formulation, at whatever level within organisations, will be expected to pay much more attention to the detail, undertaking well-executed analysis, being transparent in what they do, identifying all reasonable risks and paying attention to how they will be mitigated.

STRATEGY AUDIT

In order to improve performance you first need to understand your starting point, your strengths and weaknesses, and how each will promote or limit what you can achieve. There are two facets to this. The first is to understand what the most successful strategy teams or businesses look like, how they behave and how near your team is to emulating them. The second is to understand what it takes to lead such a team – do you personally have the necessary attributes for success?

 QUICK TIP COMPETITION
Set up a file on each of your competitors and collate the information into a common format, looking at new products launched, marketing approaches and major deals won. Most of this information, including press releases, will be available from their websites and industry publications.

Team assessment

Is my team maximising its potential to think strategically?

Use the following checklist to assess the current state of your team, considering each element in turn. Use a simple Red-Amber-Green evaluation, where Red reflects areas where you disagree strongly with

the statement and suggests there are significant issues requiring immediate attention, Amber suggests an area of concern and risk, and Green
means it is on track.

ID	CATEGORY	EVALUATION CRITERIA	STATUS
Strategy			**RAG**
STR1	Strategic planning – leadership	The team follows a defined strategy process, with clear ownership. Stakeholders work together within a common strategic framework	☐
STR2	Strategic focus	Clear objectives are set in all areas of the business, with a set of underlying assumptions and beliefs	☐
STR3	Understanding of the business environment	There is ongoing analysis of the external and competitive environments following a systematic approach that identifies market and technology trends and business impact	☐
STR4	Keeping ahead of the competition	The business has a clearly defined unique selling proposition (USP), is clear about its strategic direction and will survive and grow over the next three years.	☐
STR5	Matching key capabilities to strategic priorities	Internal processes and the structure of teams are constantly reviewed for their ability to deliver the strategy – effectively and efficiently	☐
STR6	Creating practical strategic plans	All activities required to achieve the strategic goals are identified, brought together and sequenced to one integrated and achievable plan. Business scenarios are assessed; corporate risks are identified and mitigated	☐
STR7	Commitment and ownership	All levels of the organisation are involved with the creation of strategy and provide ideas and insights. There is a strong commitment to the strategy with a 'line of sight' link between strategic goals and individual objectives	☐
STR8	Communication	Ongoing communication between all levels of the organisation is good. All staff members have a good knowledge of the plans and targets for the future and feel that they can positively influence them	☐
STR9	Culture of strategic change	There are effective change programmes in place which are supported by the	

		company culture. The goals of the overall strategy are aligned and supported by interlocked internal plans, in particular staffing and technology	☐
STR10	Performance management	Scorecards and key performance indicators (KPIs) exist for all critical areas and are regularly monitored. There is overall visibility and control of performance and key issues are resolved efficiently	☐

QUICK TIP UNDERSTANDING YOUR ORGANISATION
Put together a quiz with your team about the company and its history and test each other on how much you know.

Having identified where the gaps are in your business or team capabilities, you need to understand if you are the right person to be leading the team in the development of strategy.

CASE STORY POWER GENERATION, IAN'S STORY

Narrator Ian was a consultant working for a major European electricity generator, looking at ways for improving organisational efficiency.

Context The strategy planning department of a major European electricity generator wanted to know how they could improve organisational efficiency.

Issue Ian ran a strategy session with the board of the company and it became clear that the overwhelming problem of the company was in fact industrial relations. Any opportunity for organisational improvement depended on forming a better contract between unions and management.

Solution The board decided to hold a planning session for each of the 20 or so power stations. This brought out the real problem and forced the managers of the power stations to develop a strategy that included tackling the relationship between the unions and management. The plan included a long, hard route to fix industrial relations but was the first step in solving the problem.

Learning Strategy planning must not exclude any problems, no matter how intractable they seem. Any strategy that ignores the central issues will never succeed.

Self-assessment

Do I have what it takes?

This section presents a self-assessment checklist of the factors that make a successful Fast Track leader in strategy. These reflect knowledge, competencies, attitudes and behaviours, and highlight how these vary at different levels of the organisation. Take control of your career, behave professionally and reflect on your personal vision for the next five years. This creates a framework for action for the rest of the book.

Use the checklist opposite to identify where you personally need to gain knowledge or skills. Fill it in honestly and then get someone who knows you well, your boss or a key member of your team, to go over it with you. Be willing to change your assessment if people give you insights into yourself that you had not taken into account.

Use the following scoring process:

0 A totally new area of knowledge or skills

1 Aware of area but low knowledge and lacking skills

2 An area where you are reasonably competent and working on improvement

3 An area where you have a satisfactory level of knowledge and skills

4 An area where you are consistently well above average

5 You are recognised as a key figure in this area of knowledge and skills throughout the business

Reflect on the lowest scores and identify those areas that are critical to success. Flag them as status Red, requiring immediate attention. These will be the areas in which you have scored a 1 or 2. Identify those areas that you are concerned about and flag them as status Amber, implying areas of risk that need to be monitored closely. Those you flag as Green are areas that you consider to be good and need no immediate attention.

ID	CATEGORY	EVALUATION CRITERIA	SCORE	STATUS
Knowledge			0–5	RAG
K1	Industry and markets	Knowledge of your industry in terms of scope (boundaries), overall size and growth, and major trends. This should include an understanding of the different segments of products and markets	☐	☐
K2	Customers and competitors	Knowledge of major customers, both in terms of who they are and their wants and needs. An understanding of who the best competitors are and what they do	☐	☐
K3	Products and services	Knowledge of current products and services, including how they perform in the marketplace against their direct and indirect competitors, in particular the industry leaders	☐	☐
K4	Technologies	Insights into current and emerging technologies that will impact on future product design, access to market or process improvements	☐	☐
Competencies				
C1	Organisation and analysis	The ability to organise the different teams or individuals to identify and find the necessary information and then develop a coherent strategy	☐	☐
C2	Big-picture thinking, creativity and visioning	The ability to challenge the current status, identify and understand breakthroughs in new products, markets and process improvements. Vision and the ability to project your thinking to see what the future will look like in terms of how people will live, work and act. (This is a key area for selection and development of many large organisations)	☐	☐
C3	Scenario planning and risk management	The ability to evaluate how the future might play out and the risks that different scenarios might pose in order to choose the right strategy. An assessment of the probability and impact of different risks	☐	☐
C4	Leadership and communication	The ability to build a balanced team (including supporters and sceptics) and motivate it to work together while communicating the outcomes to the whole organisation. Leadership also means driving the process forward and facilitating discussion to identify and explore different options	☐	☐

ID	CATEGORY	EVALUATION CRITERIA	SCORE	STATUS
Attitudes			0–5	RAG
A1	Positive approach	A belief that you can make a difference and get things done – even if it means overcoming resistance from other people		
A2	Seeking synergies	The ability to find ways to combine creatively several ideas (even if they are other people's) in order to develop a new and exciting concept		
A3	Inquisitive mindset	An awareness of the need to constantly seek more effective or efficient ways of doing things. Willingness to challenge the status quo and ask why things are as they are		
A4	Breakthrough thinking	Not accepting average or second best. Constantly seeking ways to dramatically change the way things are		
Behaviours				
B1	Determination and commitment	Being prepared to see things through and persist in overcoming obstacles. Getting agreement on the process is no mean feat, let alone managing it to completion, so it is important not to be put off by early setbacks or problems		
B2	Including and encouraging others	Making it clear that you are looking for input from all parts of the organisation and are open to new ideas. This ensures the strategy will meet the needs of the whole organisation and keeps everyone focused on the output		
B3	Leading change	Understanding the need for change and recognising why others may find it difficult to take new ideas on board		
B4	Staying practical	The ability to ensure that the strategy planning does not over-analyse the current situation and that plans are created that can be delivered		

When you have looked at each of the 16 key competencies, list your scores from 0 to 5 in the boxes below, based on your assessment.

KNOWLEDGE	SCORE
K1	
K2	
K3	
K4	
Total	

COMPETENCIES	SCORE
C1	
C2	
C3	
C4	
Total	

ATTITUDES	SCORE
A1	
A2	
A3	
A4	
Total	

BEHAVIOURS	SCORE
B1	
B2	
B3	
B4	
Total	

Verify that these aggregated scores give a fair overall assessment of your strategic capabilities and then transfer them to the tables below. Next, mark where you would like your level to be in each of the 16 areas. This will help you to identify your key areas of focus.

KNOWLEDGE	ACTUAL SCORE (1–5)	REQUIRED LEVEL	STATUS (RAG)
K1 Industry and markets			
K2 Customers and competitors			
K3 Products and services			
K4 Technologies			

COMPETENCIES	ACTUAL SCORE (1–5)	REQUIRED LEVEL	STATUS (RAG)
C1 Organisation and analysis			
C2 Big picture thinking, creativity and visioning			
C3 Scenario planning and risk management			
C4 Leadership and communication			

ATTITUDES	ACTUAL SCORE (1–5)	REQUIRED LEVEL	STATUS (RAG)
A1 Positive approach			
A2 Seeking synergies			
A3 Inquisitive mindset			
A4 Breakthrough thinking			

BEHAVIOURS	ACTUAL SCORE (1–5)	REQUIRED LEVEL	STATUS (RAG)
B1 Determination and commitment			
B2 Including and encouraging others			
B3 Leading change			
B4 Staying practical			

Learning

Take a few minutes to reflect on the leadership–team effectiveness matrix below and consider your current position – where are you and what are the implications?

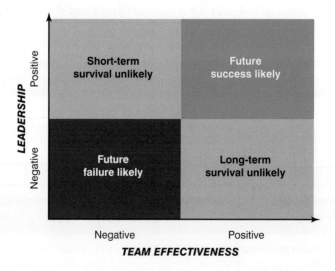

→ Bottom left – poor leadership and an ineffective team. This will result in failure. Who knows, you may already be too late.

→ **Top left – great leadership but a poor team.** You have a great vision but will be unlikely to implement it, and so it will have little impact. You will need to find a way of developing and motivating the team and introducing systems and processes to improve team effectiveness.

→ **Bottom right – poor leadership but a great team.** This implies you are highly effective and efficient as a team but may well be going in the wrong direction. It is no use being the most innovative and efficient developers of black and white televisions, to use our earlier analogy.

→ **Top right – clear leadership and direction combined with an efficient and effective team.** This is where you want to be. Lots of great new ideas for change linked to current business goals and with a team unit capable of delivering on time and within budget. You don't need this book; please give it to someone else!

STOP – THINK – ACT

Part A has given you a quick overview of what strategy is, and you will also have assessed your performance and that of your team against best practice checklists. This will have raised your awareness of what is possible and clarified where you are now.

At the end of the individual and team audits, take time to reflect on your profile in order to:

1 identify any 'quick wins' you could achieve today;

2 highlight areas to focus on in the rest of the book.

Ask yourself and the team these questions:

What should we do?	What will we change today and what difference will it make (why)? How will we know if it has been successful?
Who do we need to involve?	Who else needs to be involved to make it work and why?
What resources will we require?	What information, facilities, materials, equipment or budget will be required and are they available?
What is the timing?	When will this change be implemented – is there a deadline?

Visit **www.Fast-Track-Me.com** to use the Fast Track online planning tool.

Strategy implementation through projects

Professor Erling S. Andersen

" Projects have traditionally been seen as a way of carrying out unique tasks. This is reflected in the frequently used definition from the US Project Management Institute,[1] which says: 'A project is a temporary endeavour undertaken to create a unique product or service.'

This view of projects is still important. It reminds us that a project is way of mobilising resources to achieve a particular task, to create enthusiasm for the task and keep a clear eye on what is to be achieved. When talking about projects, a comparison is often made to the task of climbing Mount Everest. It needs a lot of preparation, detailed planning and organising, tough and fatiguing execution, and all the time a strong focus on the goal.

But projects are now considered to be much more than unique tasks. The Scandinavian School of Project Management, represented for instance by Andersen,[2] uses the following definition: 'A project is a temporary organisation, established by its base organisation to carry out an assignment on its behalf.'

This new understanding of projects enlarges the focus of project management from an operational tool to an approach for tackling the implementation of both the strategic challenges and opportunities facing top management. The project approach gives leaders of an enterprise more manoeuvrability. Previously they had to handle all challenges through the traditional line organisation, normally a functional hierarchy with complex decision-making processes and limited ability to handle problems affecting several functions of the organisation. With the new understanding they have the possibility to set up one or more temporary organisations to handle strategic problems or opportunities that they earlier had to tackle through the permanent organisation. The establishment of a temporary organisation gives them the chance to tailor-make it for the particular challenge, using people from different functions of the base organisation and perhaps even people external to the enterprise.

Top management can then link up several projects into a portfolio. This portfolio reveals the strategic agenda of top management; it shows which changes management would like to achieve and which challenges it is

[1] PMI (2004), *A Guide to the Project Management Body of Knowledge (PMBOK® Guide)*, 3rd edition, Newton Square, PA: Project Management Institute.
[2] Andersen, E.S. (2008), *Rethinking Project Management – An Organisational Perspective*, Harlow: Pearson Education.

addressing. The traditional line organisation is streamlined to run the daily operations and the ongoing projects reflect which improvements the management would like to see (for instance, the development of new products, entering into new markets, reorganising the enterprise, developing the competences of the employees or building new facilities).

It has always been a challenging job to be a project manager seeking to carry through the visions of the base organisation management. The difference now is that the success of this kind of project depends on a very close relationship and cooperation between the project manager and the project owner, i.e. the executive within the base organisation responsible for the project assignment.

The real success of a project that is supposed to help bring changes to the enterprise is not as easy to measure as the triumph at the top of Mount Everest. It is gradually revealed only as the enterprise harvests the benefits of the project.

EXPERT VOICE

PART B

BUSINESS FAST TRACK

Irrespective of your chosen function or discipline, look around at the successful managers whom you know and admire. These people are Fast Track managers – they have the knowledge and skills to perform well and fast track their careers. Notice how they excel at three things:

Tools and techniques
They have a good understanding of best practices for their particular field. This is in the form of methods and techniques that translate knowledge into decisions, insights and actions. They understand what the best companies do and have an ability to interpret what is relevant for their own role and business. The processes they use are generally simple to explain and form a logical step-by-step approach to solving a problem or capturing data and insights. They also encourage creativity – Fast Track managers do not follow a process slavishly where they know they are filling in the boxes rather than looking for insights on how to improve performance. This combination of method and creativity produces the optimum solutions.

They also have a clear understanding of what is important to know and what is simply noise. They either know this information or have it at their fingertips as and when they require it. They also have effective filtering mechanisms so that they don't get overloaded with extraneous information. The level of detail required varies dramatically from one situation to another – the small entrepreneur will work a lot more on the knowledge they have and in gaining facts from quick conversations with experts, whereas a large corporate may employ analysts and research companies. Frequently when a team is going through any process they uncover the need for further data.

Technologies
Having the facts and understanding best practice, however, will achieve little unless they are built into the systems that people use on a day-to-day

basis. Fast Track managers are good at assessing the relevance of new information technologies and adopting the appropriate ones in order to maximise both effectiveness and efficiency.

Implementation

Finally, having designed the framework that is appropriate to them and their team, Fast Track managers are also great at leading the implementation effort, putting in place the changes necessary to build and sustain the performance of the team.

How tightly or loosely you use the various tools and techniques presented in Part B will vary, and will to a certain extent depend on personal style. As you read through the following three chapters, first seek to understand how each could impact you and your team, and then decide what level of change may be appropriate, given your starting point, authority and career aspirations.

FAST TRACK TOP TEN

This chapter will help you to develop your capabilities and reputation as a strategic player in your organisation and fast track your career in the process. Success requires an understanding of strategic planning and the ability to motivate the team that will build and implement the strategy.

Here's what you will find in this chapter.

1 An explanation of the steps you need to follow to create a successful 'best practice' strategic plan.

2 Advice on how you actually implement this plan in a professional way that builds your credibility and reputation.

Setting strategy is not simple because it involves making decisions based on what might happen in the future. The problem is further compounded by the number of people happy to give advice on the subject: everyone has a view because everyone sees the future from their particular standpoint. Furthermore, even within your own environment, you may find several different methods are being used that make the task of creating one coherent plan almost impossible. And finally, even if you use the best process in the world, you still need good information in at the front end to get good results out at the back. In fact, every step must be carried out correctly for the end result to be truly valuable.

Don't be put off, though – you just need one good process that works. Think of it like building a bicycle. The steps are quite logical: start with the bike frame, add the front forks, wheels, handlebars, gears and saddle. Some aspects are fixed – for example, you couldn't add the wheels without a frame and so on – but there is still some flexibility in the order you do things. The same is true for strategy. In this book I have put forward a simple approach that includes the best and most relevant aspects of strategy.

As it turns out, I propose that you begin the process by working out your current position (the situation analysis). But equally, you could start by identifying your destination. Similarly, you could start top down (the most common), looking at high-level themes, or bottom up, starting with opportunities for improvement. The order is not crucial, but you need to get to the end of the process for it to have value. To use the bike analogy, there is no point building the whole bike and then leaving off the saddle. The good news is that the more times you do it, the more instinctive and familiar it will be. And as you continue to stay abreast of new thinking in strategy (essential to fast track your career), you can add your knowledge on to the framework you have developed here.

So what is this recommended process? Having studied more articles and books on strategy than is good for me, and implemented successful strategic plans for a wide range of companies, I propose the following steps.

→ Start the process – this is when the team comes together and agrees the steps to follow; in effect, agree a plan for making a plan (you should always try to get involved at this stage) (step 1).

→ High-level strategy – set the strategic context and high-level objectives based on the current situation (steps 2 to 4).

→ Develop the individual business unit plans if required (step 5 and 6).

→ Integrate the different plans, optimise and create one action plan (steps 7 and 8).

→ Document and communicate the plan (step 9).

→ Review regularly (step 10).

These six broad stages relate to the ten steps of this chapter, where we look at best practice and some tools and techniques to implement them successfully.

QUICK TIP **WORK FOR SOMEONE ELSE FOR A MOMENT**

Think about how you might set up a new business to compete with the one you are in. What sort of product you would build? How easy would it be to do this? Use this to understand what sets you apart as an organisation.

Remember that strategy is about defining where you would most like to be in the future based on the knowledge that you have today and this, of course, will never be perfect. Strategy is not like a mathematical problem that has one single correct answer. There will be many options available when making strategic choices. Even decisions made for the right reasons today may need to be changed because of the actions of your competition and the market. The important lesson, therefore, is not to consider strategy as a one-off process, but to ensure that it is flexible and ongoing. It must be monitored and updated over time.

The opposite is also true. Having made a clear strategic choice, it often requires the investment of time for it to deliver the promised results. Don't pull up the carrot to see if the roots are growing. Companies that are constantly changing their strategy send out confusing messages to their organisation. Employees will figure that if the strategy starts moving about, the best thing that they can do is to stay still until it has settled.

Introducing the ten-step strategy process

This chapter presents a framework of methods or techniques to improve performance and make life easier for a strategy-focused team. Each function can take a lifetime to master, but as a Fast Track manager you will know which areas to focus on – get those areas right and the team will perform.

The 'top ten' strategy tools and techniques can be remembered by ten-letter mnemonic: S-T-R-A-T-E-G-I-E-S.

1   **S**tart the process – agree the framework with the stakeholders.

2   **T**ake stock – look at how good you are and what will change in the future.

3   **R**eview high-level themes – mission, basic beliefs, competitive advantage and vision.

4   **A**gree high-level objectives.

5   **T**arget key products and markets – new product launches, new markets to address, pricing strategies and how to grow market share.

6   **E**xtend to develop internal capability and functional plans.

7   **G**enerate the risk register and 'future-proof' the plan.

8   **I**ntegrate all corporate-wide projects and key activities.

9   **E**ngage and empower the organisation with good communication.

10   **S**upervise progress and governance.

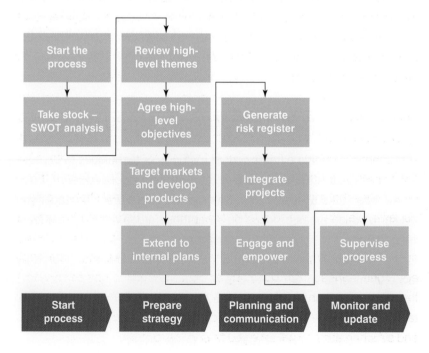

Let us look at each of these ten steps in turn.

1 STRATEGIC PLANNING PROCESS
Agree the framework with stakeholders

The first step in creating a strategy is to produce the high-level plan of action – a plan to create a plan. Whatever your role in developing strategy, you want to be involved at this stage. Find out whether your organisation already has a clear strategy planning process in place and, if so, take time to understand how it works. More often than not, though, there will not be a formal process. There can be many reasons for this, for example in a newly formed business. If this is the case, you can quickly introduce the ten-stage strategic planning process outlined in this chapter.

Once you understand the process, work with your manager and colleagues to put together a clear project plan, identifying the individual tasks and the time available to complete them. Think carefully about how much time to allocate to creating your strategy. If the time period is too short, the strategy will be based on insufficient or incorrect data or will be too vague to be of real value. If it takes too long, management will lose interest and focus on short-term urgent operational issues instead. Not only that, but the initial assumptions of your plan will quickly become out of date, causing a loss of credibility with decision makers.

One of the key success factors in developing plans is to understand what the 'outputs' or 'deliverables' should be. These are the documents, spreadsheets, reports and so on that you will create as you work through your planning process and analysis. They should be directly relevant to the final strategy document and may even form part of it. Only spend time on activities that make a specific contribution to your final strategy output. For example, don't spend a lot of time analysing data when the general conclusions are already known. There will be plenty to do without making additional work for yourself. The format of this final deliverable – the 'strategy' itself – varies from company to company. Some companies have their strategy written in a narrative report style, some in the form of presentation slides. There is no right or wrong answer, but knowing the format and structure early on will save you time in the long run.

The second step in creating a strategic plan is to identify your key stakeholders. A stakeholder is someone who is affected by the outcome of what you are doing – someone who holds a 'stake' in a successful result. Stakeholders will often include senior management, customers, suppliers, shareholders and employees. Some stakeholders will have a bigger stake than others, so it is worth spending time to understand which are the most important. Differentiate between real stakeholders and those who are just interested or supportive. Involving too many people will slow the process down, as you spend time trying to find a consensus of opinion, rather than making the right decision.

Put together a provisional list and arrange to meet with each of the stakeholders individually and as soon as possible. Remember that first impressions are important at these meetings. Prepare well and, if possible, take a colleague with you who can help with additional questions and taking notes. Use these first meetings to explain and refine the strategy process. Take time to fully understand the stakeholder's motivations and objectives and, if possible, get a commitment as to how much time they will have to help you. When your meeting has ended, copy up the minutes of the meeting and send them out within 24 hours. It is important to keep all stakeholders regularly updated with your thinking – starting that process with your first meeting will set a good impression. When you update your stakeholders, they will be interested in your latest thinking, the basis of that thinking and the progress of the final strategy outputs, so be sure to have this information prepared in a clear format.

2 TAKE STOCK *Analysing your position*

It is difficult to chart your path to the future if you are not clear on your starting point. Step 2 of the strategy process is about understanding where you are today and the pressures your business faces. There are five broad stages to this.

1 Assess the needs of your customers and how well you meet those needs.

2 Evaluate the competition and your industry, and understand the relative strengths and weaknesses of your products.

3 Analyse the efficiency of your organisation, looking at the key internal processes and the supply chain.

4 Review the macro environment so that you understand the key external factors that affect your organisation and their impact in the future.

5 Summarise your findings.

Understanding your customers

Your first port of call should be to your customers and potential customers. In order to build customer loyalty and in turn market share, you must understand their buying criteria and how well you meet their needs. Customer needs normally break down into four areas – product, processes, people and price.

> **QUICK TIP WHY, OH WHY?**
> Get into the habit of asking 'Why?'. Why is this product the way it is, why do we go to market in the way we do?

Let us take the example of a mobile phone.

1 **Product.** Buying criteria might include the weight or size of the phone; they might also include particular features such as fast internet access or a high-quality camera.

2 **Process.** Criteria might include how easy it is to connect a customer to the phone network, to add a new service or speak directly to a customer support person.

3 **People.** Customers might consider that it is important for staff to be knowledgeable on a range of subjects or empowered to solve their problems first time.

4 **Price.** Pricing criteria might include the cost of buying the handset up front, monthly payment terms or the option of different pricing plans.

Think of your own top ten buying criteria and identify at least one criterion in each of the four areas described. Then, from your list, ask customers to rate each area in turn on how important it is to them and how well you score against it. Although you are measuring different things, by scoring each out of 10 (for example, a 10 in customer care means friendly and helpful, whereas a 10 for pricing probably means cheap), your products are services will hopefully be scoring highly in those areas that are important to your customers.

 QUICK TIP **WHAT DO YOUR CUSTOMERS THINK?**
Set up a 'valued customer group' to maintain an up-to-date view of what customers are looking for. Invite customers that also use competitors' products, to get a broad range of feedback.

It makes eminent sense, of course, to ask the customer what their ideal would be for each of the buying criteria – in other words, what would you have to do to get a score of 10 out of 10? It is not uncommon at this stage for businesses to realise that they are providing something for customers (sometimes at great expense) that the customer doesn't value. Take the opportunity to ask how you compare with your competitors. And finally, find out how their needs might change in the future and what improvements they would like to see.

Draw up a table like the example below to show the scores in each area:

	CRITERIA	CUSTOMER IDEAL	IMPORTANCE TO CUSTOMER (OUT OF 10)	HOW THEY RATE YOU (OUT OF 10)
Product	Quality	Zero faults	7	6
	Range	Meets all requirements	8	5
	Ease of use	Inituitive (stable)	9	5
Process	Flexibility of ordering	Tailor solution to each need	6	8
	Reliability of delivery	Same day every time	7	7
	Account administration	Goes unnoticed	7	4

People	Knowledge of sales staff	All staff know all products and their application	7	8
	Ability to solve technical questions	First time fix every time	8	7
Price	Competitive	Lowest price	8	7
	Discount schemes	Reward customer loyalty properly	5	7

This assessment can be carried out with face-to-face meetings or through a carefully prepared customer survey. Focus groups can be very helpful in providing additional information that cannot always be gleaned from a questionnaire. Focus group members will usually be supportive of your company and the products you make. They will give you a subjective view of what makes a good product, helping you to fill in the gaps in your market knowledge. Think carefully about who you include in your assessment. In general terms you are measuring how well your product fits the needs of a particular market. You will not be able to get a daily update from your focus group, so you may wish to consider other ways of gathering information on an ongoing basis, perhaps using sales and customer care interactions to collect the relevant statistics. Working on these assessments is a good way to get involved in the strategy process, either collecting the information, or better still working with colleagues to draft the questionnaire.

While you are collecting information on the strengths and weaknesses of a particular product, think about the background of the target audience and ask whether they have the same needs – in marketing terms, people with different needs will be part of a different market segment. It is important to understand the different market segments that your product addresses. To take our mobile phone example, if you ask a young audience what is important, you will get answers about look and feel and style. Ask a business audience and you will get answers around peak call rates and email or data access. Ask an older audience and you will probably get answers around ease of use. In other words, the same product will get different scores when you ask different market segments.

There are different ways that you can break down a market into segments. Look at different options and choose one that fits your business.

Examples of different segmentations include age (as with the example above), geography (looking at the needs of different regions or countries) and value (looking at the market according to customer value or income). Even within the same market segment, it is important to verify that the sample is representative. Consider changing the members of your focus group on a regular basis so that you get new ideas and opinions.

Once you have divided your target audience into valid market segments, it should be straightforward enough to measure how important the different buying criteria are to each segment. Plot these values on to a chart, or what is sometimes called a 'strategic canvas'[1] or 'perceived use value' graph. An example of a strategic canvass is shown in the figure below. If you have sufficient information about your competitors, you may also wish to plot where they are on the canvass.

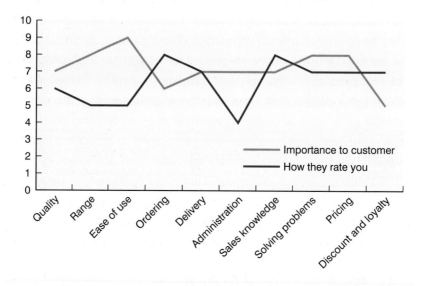

In the example above, which uses the values from the previous table, you can see that having products that are easy to use is the most important criterion. This is one of the weakest areas of the product, so it would obviously be an area of focus in the strategy. Secondly, the administration process is considered very poor by the customer and, although this is not a top priority, it should also be addressed. In contrast, the

[1]Kim, W.C. and Mauborgne, R. (2002), 'Charting your company's future', *Harvard Business Review*, June, 77–83.

company exceeds expectations in sales knowledge and discount schemes. The discount scheme in particular might be something to look at. It seems at first glance that discounts are being offered to customers who don't consider them particularly important.

Understanding your competition and industry

However well you meet your customers' expectations, you will only be successful if your performance exceeds that of the competition. Take the time to analyse your competitors to identify the potential opportunities and threats they may present. Start by doing some background work, looking at their websites, reviewing their brochures and promotional material or visiting their stand at a trade fair. You can also include the feedback from your customer reviews as discussed in the previous section. Ask your customers to compare you to your competitors for the top ten buying criteria. You may find that some of your competitors are more successful with certain types of customer. As part of your analysis, look for the characteristics that these customers have in common with each other. Try to find out which of the buying criteria are of particular importance to this group.

QUICK TIP **PUT YOURSELF IN THEIR SHOES**
Imagine you are working for a competitor and develop their strategy. Use this to highlight vulnerabilities in your current position. What do you think they would say about you in terms of what you do well and what you don't?

The simple economics of supply and demand suggest that if you have a large number of competitors in your market, your profitability will go down. If your business has been established for a long time, the chances are that you probably know your main competitors quite well. However, in 1980, Michael Porter[2] suggested that it isn't just the immediate competitors that put pressure on profitability. In fact, as shown in the diagram overleaf, he identified five key forces altogether that exert an influence. The five forces are:

[2]Porter, M.E. (1979), 'How competitve forces shape strategy', *Harvard Business Review*, March/April.

1 direct competition

2 the threat of new entrants

3 the threat of substitute products or services

4 the bargaining power of suppliers

5 the bargaining power of customers.

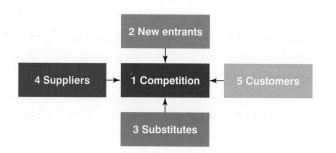

SOURCE: PORTER, M.E. (1979). REPRODUCED WITH PERMISSION.

It follows, then, that if you want to develop a robust strategy, you need to think about possible new competitors too. These businesses will often focus on niches within your target market and can be very successful because of their agility and low overheads. Look also for substitute competitors. These are organisations that typically provide completely different products but which satisfy the same need of the customer. For example, a restaurant may not be a direct competitor to a cinema, but it does compete for the same entertainment cash. The five forces theory also encourages organisations to look at their supply chain. To maximise leverage and profitability, you want to be able to choose from a range of suppliers. Conversely, you want to be one of only a few suppliers that can provide goods to your customers.

Once you have a full picture of the different types of competitor, it is worth summarising the opportunities and threats that this brings. If you have a significant advantage over competitors in one of the key buying criteria, you may want to exploit it in your strategy. Similarly, if you are at a disadvantage in any area, you will need to counter this threat to your business with a plan of action. And don't forget, while you are making strides to exploit your advantages and mitigate the threats, your competitors are doing the same to you.

Assessing your skills and capabilities

Everything you do must be competitive to maintain success. If you use the analogy of football (a lot of top strategic thinkers use analogies), all 11 players have an important part to play. You cannot expect to win without a goalkeeper, for example. In the same way, everything you do should give you some sort of competitive advantage, whether it is improving sales, reducing cost or improving quality. This includes internal activities too, such as new product development, customer operations, manufacturing, distribution, human resources, finance, procurement and IT – in short, any function that is not directly involved in the sales process. Each internal department needs to canvass feedback from the rest of the organisation to ensure its goals and activities are correctly aligned. This can be done through face-to-face meetings with key managers from each department, or with a carefully written survey if you need to canvass a wider response. Benchmarking can also help to give statistical information on how well a particular function is performing. In the world of IT, for example, there are several industry-specific groups that can provide precise and relevant comparison data. Be careful how you use benchmarks, and if your organisation is to be compared to others, favourably or otherwise, be sure to seek an explanation of the differences.

QUICK TIP **HOW DO THE BEST IN THE BUSINESS DO IT?**
Make a list of the most innovative companies you know and ask what it is that really excites you about them, and what they do differently.

Strategic planning is often a good opportunity to review business processes. Start by listing your key processes and try to work out the cost of each transaction. To take a simple (and perhaps rather crude) example, supposing a purchasing organisation raises 1,000 purchase orders per annum with a staff of four at a cost of £100,000. If this was all the procurement department did, you could calculate the cost of raising each purchase order as £100. Whether or not you consider this to be high is another matter, but understanding the process and its related cost will help you develop a plan for improvement.

Examining other influences

There are many influences beyond the priorities of your customers and the strength of your competition that may affect your success. These tend not to relate to any particular competitive environment, but they can have an equally important effect on success. These general environment factors are sometimes summarised in the acronym PESTEL – standing for political, economic, social, technological, environmental and legislative.

Either on your own or in a workshop with your team, think about the opportunities and threats that each one might bring. Use the table below to get you started.

AREA OF INFLUENCE	OUTLINE OF THE KEY ISSUES	POSSIBLE OPPORTUNITIES	POSSIBLE THREATS
Political influences	Political influences may include the cost of doing business in certain areas	Government-sponsored business initiatives	Governments demanding a share of key businesses in key sectors, e.g. oil or mineral reserves
Economic trends	Look for issues that may have significant impact, for example, interest rate changes. If your business is international, you will need to understand the influence of currency fluctuations. If you are reliant on transport, you may need to look at the predicted trends for oil prices	Interest rate falls, favourable currency rates	Interest rate rises, unfavourable currency rates, increases in the price of oil
Social trends	Social trends may affect where your customers are based and the working practices of your employees	Customers moving to new business areas, employees wanting to work from home, corporate social responsibility	Employees working in remote locations, requesting flexible working practices
Technology trends	Technology has changed the landscape of business and the way we work. New technologies can completely erase long-established businesses and need to be considered on an ongoing basis	Reduced cost of computing, ability to work in remote locations via broadband and VPN links, other new applications of science and technology	New technologies replacing existing established products in a very short time

Envirnomental trends	With a strong trend towards environmental issues, you need to consider the impact your organisation has on the environment, and the possible effect this might have on business	Improving the carbon footprint of your organisation, recycling initiatives, etc.	Adverse effects of manufacturing by-products, carbon emissions
Legislative and political influences	All businesses are affected by changes in legislation to improve financial accountability and protect customers	Financial and technical consulting	Changes to data protection, financial reporting (such as Sarbanes-Oxley) and changes to agricultural policy

Summarising your current situation

At the end of your customer analysis, you will have a better understanding of how your products are used and appreciated by your customers. You will know which attributes are important to which customers. You will have compared yourself against your competition and you will be aware of the strengths and weaknesses of your business processes. With this clear picture of your starting point and the environment you are working in, you will soon be in good shape to craft some high-level themes and your strategic destination.

This first stage of developing your strategy is very important. It is important to invest time to ensure that the information you gather is accurate and that your analysis is sufficiently detailed. Be wary of having too much statistical information though. Strategy, is of course, the 'art of the general' and it makes sense to summarise the information. If you can do this in table or chart form, so much the better. It can also be helpful to use one of the simple tools of the strategist – the SWOT analysis. You are probably familiar with SWOT (strengths, weaknesses, opportunities and threats). One of the first strategic planning sessions I was involved in was for a French company. I was surprised that they used this method when there were so many other techniques available. But the more strategy planning projects I have worked on, the more I have come to understand that summarising strategic positions in one place is valuable – and SWOT lets you do this.

QUICK TIP *CREATE A 'SUPER-COMPETITOR' MONSTER*
Make a list of the top ten items from your competitors that you would like in your company. Develop a 'super-competitor' that has all of these best features. What would it look like? How would you build this kind of organisation for yourself?

Summarise your strengths and weaknesses from the work you did with your customers, understanding what you do well and what you don't (see figure below). Focus on the areas that your customers see value in. For example, having a customer loyalty scheme might seem like a good idea, but it is only worthwhile if it increases the loyalty of customers!

Strengths	Weaknesses
What is the organisation really good at – in the eyes of the customer and relative to the competition?	What needs to be improved – in the eyes of the customer and relative to the best competition?
Opportunities	**Threats**
What could improve business performance – looking at new markets, technology, social, political and economic trends?	What could damage sales in the future – looking at new competitiors, substitutes and existing competitors as well as other influences?

Try to get a balance between strengths and weaknesses. Some cultures find it difficult to talk openly about company weaknesses but it is important to have a balanced view. Listing everything as a strength might make people feel better at the meeting, but it won't count for much when your competition eats you for lunch.

3 STRATEGIC CONTEXT

It's now time to do some preliminary work on the strategic context. The aim of this stage is to give guidance about the nature and future of the company. It uses what we learnt in the previous section to avoid creating unrealistic objectives. For example, you wouldn't want to pin your future success on delivering excellent customer care if your organisation is currently languishing at the bottom of the customer care 'league table'.

There are five areas that will help you define your 'strategic context'.

1 Your statement of mission – what you do.

2 Target products and markets – describing which products you sell to which markets.

3 Competitive advantage – what makes you stand out as a company (and whether this will endure).

4 Basic beliefs – your assumptions of change affecting your company in your market.

5 Values – the culture of the organisation.

Your company's mission

To explain clearly what a company does, and sometimes how it plans to do it, many large organisations develop what is known as a mission statement. A mission statement would not normally set goals or targets – we come on to this in step 4 – but merely explains what the company does and will continue to do as it goes forward. In some ways it acts as an anchor for the company, providing reassurance of where the business focus is and will be in the future. Mission statements are often quite general statements and for this reason keep their relevance for a long period of time. The longer they stay relevant, the more they also start to represent the culture of the company.

You can see in the examples of Coca-Cola and HSBC in the table overleaf that their mission statements describe not only what the organisation does today, but also what it hopes to continue doing into the future – 'create value' and 'leading in our chosen markets', for example. HSBC in particular has withstood significant market turbulence by maintaining ethical lending levels. Both statements contain expressions that relate to the culture of the companies.

COMPANY	MISSION STATEMENT	SOURCE
Coca-Cola	Everything we do is inspired by our enduring mission: To refresh the world ... in body, mind, and spirit. To inspire moments of optimism ... through our brands and our actions. To create value and make a difference ... everywhere we engage.	**www.coca-cola.com**
HSBC	Leading in our chosen markets. Delivering an outstanding client experience based on excellence in sales, services and solutions. Achieving a superior, ethically based, long-term return for our shareholders. Building highly motivated, high-performance teams. Creating a challenging, rewarding and fun work environment.	**www.hsbc.com**

High-level target products and markets

Either as an addition or as a complement to the mission statement, it is often helpful to make a clear statement at a high level about which products you will offer to which markets. To do this, first, think about the broad markets you intend to address and the type of products you will offer in each one. Unless you are looking to diversify into a completely different business, this will include your current markets and the future ones you wish to target. Put together a summarising statement, for example:

'Our target market is for in-country training services in the US, diversifying to chosen international markets in the next two years.'

'Our target market is consumers of printer supplies focusing on small businesses, with a view to extending our range of office products.'

'Our target market is wealthy customers of luxury goods across Europe and Asia.'

These three statements may seem relatively straightforward, but they can take some time to create, as it is important for everyone to be in agreement. In step 5 we do further analysis as to exactly which products we should sell into which markets.

Statement of competitive advantage

Good strategy tells you how to position your business to be successful and grow. To achieve this, you need to be better than the competition, not just now but into the future. You do not have to be 'the best and the cheapest and the fastest', just the right combination. Understanding what your competitive advantage is today is the first step to maintaining it in the future. It may be that in some markets you cannot find any clear competitive advantage today, let alone in the future. If this is the case, check again with your key customers. If you are still unconvinced, decide quickly whether to improve your competitive position or pull out of the market. Some products just take too much effort to sell and therefore if you have one of these, you should get rid of it and find a replacement. Unlike sporting competitions, customers do not normally give a prize for second place.

Now take the analysis from the previous section, and identify your strengths across the business. Rank your strengths in order of the competitive advantage they each deliver – in other words, how important are these criteria in helping customers choose to buy from you rather than from someone else (if at all)? Next, look at how easy it will be to maintain competitive advantage in the future. There are many factors to consider when it comes to competitive advantage – for example, how easy will it be for competitors to copy, how easy will it be for new competitors to come into the market and how long will this advantage remain valuable for customers?

Using the example in the table overleaf of a company that sells computer training, you can see how it is looking to maintain its competitive advantage in the future.

This exercise should be helpful in many ways. It will challenge some of your beliefs in terms of why your customers buy from you, and it may contradict what you found in your detailed analysis. Use a balance of facts and instinct in making your choices. When you complete your strategy, this should give you confidence that you have a sustainable competitive advantage.

COMPETITIVE ADVANTAGE	IMPORTANCE	IMPORTANCE IN THE FUTURE	FACTORS IN MAINTAINING THIS ADVANTAGE
Our courses have been developed over a long period and are ranked highly by delegates	1	1	Course content needs to be updated regularly based on feedback from our key customers and knowledge of new computer products
Our course facilities are extremely well suited to learning and are advanced technically	2	3	We need to keep the facilities up to date and maintain an effective learning environment
Our trainers are the best in the industry	3	2	Recruitment and retention of highly qualified trainers is essential, as we could easily lose key expertise

Statement of beliefs

Creating a list of basic beliefs is the next stage in setting your strategic context. These are the principles that the senior management believes will continue to hold true in the lifetime of the strategic plan. These will play a key role in shaping your strategy. Put together a list of anything that you think will act as a guide for the future. Include statements about market potential in different areas, customer buying patterns, work practices or the impact of environmental change, and make them specific to your business context. Against each of your beliefs, list the evidence that exists to support each one. Be wary of basing a strategy on a set of beliefs for which there is little or no concrete evidence.

The example in the table below uses our training company example and identifies a number of beliefs that are the foundation of building the strategic plan with supporting evidence.

BELIEF	EVIDENCE
We believe that the training market will remain buoyant for the next three years	Market predictions, which say that technology will be increasingly important for companies and there is a corresponding shortfall in qualified staff
We believe that our key competitive advantage is the quality of our courses and the facilities we use to run them	Our feedback from customers after the course completion and follow-up discussions. An independent benchmark carried out earlier in the year

We believe that customers will look for new and innovative training courses and will want to continue to attend courses on-site	Feedback from customers and trends in the industry. Distance learning will be important in some areas, but not in the highly technical courses we run
We will continue to specialise in technology training and will not diversify to general management training	All our courses are technology based and our facilities set up for multi-user training. General management training is highly competitive and would require new trainers, a new learning approach and a modification of our facilities

Developing a statement of values

For a company to be successful over a long period of time, it needs to protect its reputation and act with integrity. For a small company, it is easy for employees to feel the culture of the organisation and behave according to the values of the senior management. However, as a company grows, it becomes more difficult to understand what those values are and the behaviour it should exhibit. For this reason, many larger organisations develop a set of values that guide employees in their day-to-day activities. These 'value statements' are often published as part of the corporate strategy and help define the culture of an organisation. Companies invest time and money to ensure that all new and existing employees understand fully these values, their implications and why they are an important part of the culture and success of that company. Often it is the founder of the company who creates the list of the company's values, as they describe what sort of company they want it to be. Bill Hewlett and Dave Packard created their set of values for Hewlett-Packard (HP); this value set subsequently became known as 'the HP Way'. It is taught to all those who join the company and is used as a guide to all business behaviour.

The table overleaf shows how two of the world's leading companies have captured the culture and integrity of their organisation in their statements of values. Both these value statements have come from their respective company websites, providing further proof of their desire to promote and communicate these value sets.

BP	IBM
BP has the following values as guides for practical action: → To have the best competitive corporate, operating and financial performance. → To improve, and to be accessible, inclusive and diverse. → To engage the creative talents of our employees, and develop and apply leading, cost-effective technology and intellectual creativity to enhance innovation and new ideas. → To carry on our business in an environmentally responsible manner, and develop cleaner energy and renewable energy sources. The group is committed to the responsible treatment of the planet's resources, and to the development of sources of lower-carbon energy. Source: **www.bp.com**	There is a set of fundamental principles which guide IBM management in the conduct of their business. Interestingly, in 2007, the company invited all 319,000 IBMers around the world to review the core values that had been in place since the company's foundation. In the end, IBM workers themselves determined that their actions would be driven by these values: → Dedication to every client's success. → Innovation that matters, for our company and for the world. → Trust and personal responsibility in all relationships. In the words of Samuel J. Palmisano, Chairman, President and Chief Executive Officer: *I must tell you, this process has been very meaningful to me. We are getting back in touch with what IBM has always been about – and always will be about – in a very concrete way. And I feel that I've been handed something every CEO craves: a mandate, for exactly the right kinds of transformation, from an entire workforce.* Source:**www.ibm.com/ibm/values/us**

QUICK TIP WHY ARE WE DIFFERENT?

Ask your team what it is they admire most about the organisation – what are the aspects of behaviour and other aspects that help to define the culture? What are the values and behaviours that set you apart?

If your company does not have a statement of values, think carefully about how, and indeed if, this would help. If you are part of the strategy team, find out what your colleagues think. Work together to create your own value statements using the two examples above as a guide. To be effective, it should be done as a team exercise. Try not to be too idealistic, but rather stay with what is realistic. Don't forget that someone will have to stand in front of the organisation and explain it. For this reason, be sure to give the evidence for those values you list. For example, it would not make sense to emphasise 'employee development' as a core value if there has been no training budget for the last three years or if all senior management positions are recruited from outside the company.

It is also worth reflecting on why companies consider values so important. To some extent, it has been a key driver of the development of strategic thinking over the years. It started with Pascale and Athos,[3] who identified seven key levers available to management to deliver success. In their 7-S model shown below, they noted that Japanese companies gave particular attention to the four 'soft' levers, namely staff, skills, style and shared values.

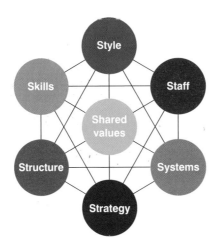

In his book, *What is Strategy and Does it Matter?*,[4] Richard Whittington talks about how strategy has evolved, moving from a centralised or internally driven process to one that takes more consideration of the market, its people and ultimately society as a whole. This has been a response to understanding the importance of customers and employees who now have much better market knowledge and a higher mobility than before. And that makes it all the more important to give special consideration to loyalty. It doesn't just make people feel better, it makes good business sense.

[3] Pascale, Richard Tanner and Athos, Antony J. (1986), *The Art of Japanese Management*, Harmondsworth: Penguin.
[4] Whittington, Richard (2000), *What is Strategy and Does it Matter?*, London: Cengage Learning.

A final word on strategic context

Spending time developing your values, beliefs and a mission statement will provide much needed guidance, not only for what will be done, but also for what won't. This is always a difficult concept, particularly for those who are risk averse. People intuitively want to keep a range of options open if they are not sure which ones will succeed. Think of it like specialising in an Olympic event however. If you enter the weightlifting competition and the marathon, you will be forever undecided as to how to train and will probably end up failing in both. In contrast, if you were good at running the 100 metres, you could easily consider entering the 200 metres. For your own business, you need to agree where skills and markets are complementary and where they detract from each other and then set your strategy accordingly. If you have issues like this, it is important to resolve them early in the strategic process.

Another point relates to versatility. As we have seen, many large organisations have mission and value statements. They provide focus, reassurance and a common purpose. Large companies need this more than small companies, where employees are often in different locations and there is a stronger need to unite them under a common theme. Large companies, by nature of their size, are less able to make radical change and it is therefore often more appropriate for them to create statements that endure for longer. Smaller companies have the opposite perspective. Their ability to move quickly is often a key competitive advantage. If you work in a medium or small company, you need to consider how to create statements that do not restrict your options for manoeuvre. Indeed, you could even decide not to have one at all.

Finally, it is important that you don't get hung up on what to call your statements, or feel you have to separate them as I have in this chapter. There are no hard rules as to what you include in your mission statement or any other statement. Some argue that the mission statement should contain a formulation of objectives, others that it differentiates the company from its competitors. For example, the first sentence of PepsiCo's mission (source **www.pepsico.com**), 'To be the world's premier consumer products company focused on convenient foods and beverages', is making a clear statement about the future position of the company.

Now we have reached the end of this step in the process, you should have a clear view of the following.

1 A summary of what you do as a company.

2 A high-level view of which markets you address today and will address in the future.

3 An understanding of what sets you apart from your competition in these markets.

4 The behaviour and values that are important to succeed.

The next stage is to set yourself some targets.

4 TOP-LEVEL OBJECTIVES

There are two steps in developing your top-level objectives.

1 Creation of a high-level statement, summarising your aspirations – the vision.

2 Agreement of the main goals that need to be achieved – the high-level objectives.

Vision statement

In the previous two steps we looked at your current performance and developed a context in terms of the values that will guide you in formulating strategy. We are now ready to define the destination. This is one of the most difficult parts of strategy – creating a high-level overarching objective. There are many different ways to do this and, in fact, entire books have been written on the subject. The following table contains three examples of vision statements from internationally recognised companies.

COMPANY	VISION	SOURCE
Avis	To be the country's premier transport service provider in the car rental industry by delivering global quality services to our customers.	www.avis.com.ph

COMPANY	VISION	SOURCE
Barclays	We are committed to building a world-class organisation. We aspire to be amongst the most valuable and admired financial services companies in the world: → A business that leads in its chosen markets. → A portfolio of brands that is synonymous with quality and integrity. → A culture based on high performance and behavioural excellence.	www.barclays.com
Marks and Spencer	To be the standard against which all others are measured.	www2.marksand spencer.com

Vision statements are less common than the mission statements we discussed in the previous step. In fact, companies often combine their future intentions within their mission statement, as we saw with the example of PepsiCo: 'To be the world's premier consumer products company focused on convenient foods and beverages.'

The aim of the vision statement should be to describe what the organisation will look like and have achieved in the future. It is an aspirational goal, but one that is measurable in some way. In my experience, vision statements are useful for organisations in developing a common purpose. However, to provide more immediate and clear purpose, I recommend some guidelines to create a very specific high-level goal. This type of vision statement is sometimes referred to as a 'statement of purpose'. It should contain:

→ the strategic time frame, say two, five or ten years;

→ an objective and the units used to measure it;

→ suggestions on how this objective will be achieved by emphasising core competencies.

Like any objective, it should conform to the SMART criteria – specific, measurable, achievable, realistic and timed. For example:

'In two years, we aim to be the largest training company in the Gulf region measured by profitability.'

'To be one of the top 100 fastest growing companies in Germany by 2010.'

'We will use our construction expertise to grow revenue in our housing business by 20 per cent and diversify to commercial property within five years.'

'A successful and cost-effective IT department as measured by user feedback and budget performance.'

The last example shows how you can create a vision statement at a functional level as well as company level.

Think about what your statement of purpose would be. As a way of getting started, consider three or four important measures of business success and set a target against each one. In the first example above, the training company might have considered customer feedback, revenue and profitability as their top three measures of performance. Customer feedback could have been the most important if the company was looking to improve course quality or increase market share by building an excellent reputation. Revenue might have been chosen, encouraging the company to run more courses, but perhaps at a lower profit margin. As it turned out, the company chose profitability as its key measure because it felt that this was the best driver of good business practice, requiring a careful selection of course portfolio, good cost management and professional sales.

Once you have chosen your most important measure, you need to set a target against it. This can be an absolute number, a percentage improvement or a comparison with the competition. In our training example, the company used a comparison target, measuring themselves against all national competitors in their market sector. Convert your statement into an objective, giving it one last check against the SMART criteria above. It is particularly important that this statement of purpose stretches the organisation but remains achievable.

High-level strategic objectives

The next step is to expand your top-level objective into more granular objectives that are meaningful for all employees. You should consider all the measures that drive your business and set targets for them.

High-level objectives can relate to revenue growth, customer satisfaction, higher profits, better staff retention or improved operational efficiency. Whatever the targets, they must be realistic. If they are too aggressive, they will not be supported, or will require the company to take unreasonable risks. Make them too easy and the company will grow complacent, eventually losing its competitiveness. You will instinctively know if you need a bold change of direction, requiring aggressive growth and improved performance. If you do, this boldness needs to be expressed in terms of high-level objectives.

In theory, it is possible to align the company to meet any single objective. The problem comes when two objectives conflict with each other. For example, trying to double sales revenue but not investing in additional salespeople; or doubling profitability and expecting customer satisfaction to improve. In their book, *The Balanced Scorecard*, Kaplan and Norton[5] explain that companies need a broad range of objectives in each of four areas to be successful. These four areas are customer, internal process, people and financial results.

1 On the **customer** side, targets might relate to new product launches, market share, new business levels, new market development goals and sales targets.

2 On the **process** side, targets might relate to improving customer care (for example, call answer time, fix rates for solving customer problems), order delivery cycles and so on.

3 On the **people** side, targets might relate to staff retention or employee satisfaction.

4 On the **financial** side, targets might include profitability targets, cost reduction and profit margin. Remember, if you are setting bold targets, don't forget to check back that your strategic plans support them in terms of new initiatives, resources and financial investment.

Your top-level objectives help quantify what success looks like. Be wary of publishing them too early. It is normally better to wait until you have worked through the rest of your strategy before going public, or you run the risk of setting goals that are either too difficult or too easy – and then causing confusion when you change them.

[5]Kaplan, Robert S. and Norton, David P. (1996), *The Balanced Scorecard: Translating Strategy into Action*, Boston, MA: Harvard Business School Press.

5 TARGET KEY PRODUCTS INTO CHOSEN MARKETS

As we have found in previous steps, strategy is about focus, paying special attention to areas that will deliver increased benefit and spending less time on those that don't. So the question is, 'Which products should we sell to which markets to deliver the best result?' To find out, we need answers to the following three questions:

1 How far do we need to move from selling our existing products to our current markets?

2 Where are the best product and market opportunities?

3 Where should we put our 'strategic emphasis'?

Market or resource driven?

It is worth mentioning at this point that there are two possible approaches – a market approach and a resource approach. With the market approach, the business is interested in the best opportunities that exist in the market. They first look for the opportunities and then they develop the capabilities – hopefully enhancing what they have, rather than starting from scratch. This is called a market-driven strategy (MDS).[6] But equally, there are companies that believe their competitive advantage comes from the uniqueness of their resources (e.g. manufacturing plants, a multi-national sales force). Their view is, 'How can we make the best use of what we have?' This is the resource-based view (RBV). These two approaches may come up with different answers. You might want to keep them both in mind when you determine the scope of your products and markets.

How big and how risky?

There is generally a trade-off to be made in terms of growth and risk – in other words, the greater the required growth, the greater the likely risk. So, if there is a large 'planning gap' – i.e. a large difference between where

[6]De Wit, B. and Meyer, R. (1999) *Strategy Synthesis*, London: Cengage Learning.

you are today and what you want to achieve in terms of results – you will probably have to take more risk in developing your products and markets.

Igor Ansoff[7] developed what is known as the 'Ansoff growth vector', a 2 × 2 matrix for evaluating different growth strategies. The figure below is an extended version of this. It shows current products, modified products (e.g. improved products, replacement products and product line extensions) and new products along one axis. The other axis shows current markets, extended markets (e.g. new customers in current markets) and new markets. This matrix highlights five potential options for growth, each with different levels of risk. Generally, the further away from the top left cell, the greater the risk.

1 Business as usual (BAU) – providing more emphasis to existing products in existing markets to increase market share.

2 New product development (NPD) – modifying existing products or developing new ones to serve existing markets.

3 New market development (NMD) – selling existing products to extended markets or into new markets.

4 New business development (NBD) – selling modified products to extended/new markets or selling modified/new products into an extended market.

5 Diversification – selling new products to new markets.

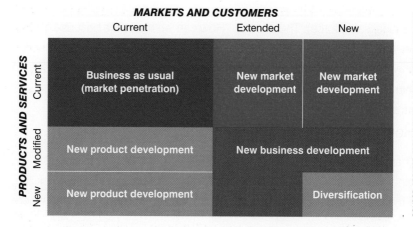

[7]Ansoff, I. (1957), 'Strategies of diversification', *Harvard Business Review*, Sept/Oct, 113–24.

This is the very heart of strategic thinking. You will have many options to consider and it will require all of your creative and analytical powers to identify and evaluate all the different possibilities. Of course, if you are well placed in your existing 'business as usual' activities, you would not necessarily move beyond what you do today. But if you have limited competitive advantage and there are threats to the market, you will need to look further afield. Look carefully at each of the different options as they will have wide-ranging implications for success and the resources required. This analysis identifies your 'strategic thrust'. It should be consistent with your aspirational goals and high-level objectives.

Segmenting products and markets

A new 'strategic thrust' usually requires you to rethink how you divide up (or segment) your products and markets. There are many ways to do this. For example, markets can be segmented by geography (e.g. Europe, North America, Asia) or by customer demographics (e.g. age or income). It is important that the segmentation is mutually exclusive (i.e. no overlap between segments) and collectively exhaustive (i.e. all market segments are included).[8]

Products can also be segmented in different ways. Electrical retailers, for example, group washing machines, fridges, dishwashers and so on together as white goods, and TVs, videos and hi-fi as brown goods. Products in a similar group should share common characteristics. Think about your own product and market groupings. You may need to experiment a few times with your segmentation to get the most sense out of the result.

Using the example in the figure overleaf, think about how you would draw up a product market matrix for your environment. Consider your presence (P) and the market attractiveness (A) for each cell. Attractiveness is dependent on the following two factors.

1 **The attractiveness of the market itself**. Factors that make a market attractive might include high market growth, strong customer demand, entry barriers and government action.

---

[8] 'Mutually exclusive, collectively exhaustive' or 'MECE' (pronounced 'me see') is an analytical technique used by McKinsey Consulting and described by Rasiel, Ethan (1999), *The McKinsey Way*, New York: McGraw-Hill Professional.

2 **The strength of your competitive position.** Factors to consider include existing market share, weak competition, good products and production capability.

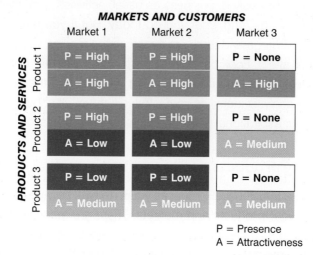

MARKETS AND CUSTOMERS

P = Presence
A = Attractiveness

In this example, the market presence and attractiveness is marked for each product/market cell in turn. You can see that the company has a strong presence for products 1 and 2 in markets 1 and 2. There is currently no product in market 3, but the markets are reasonably attractive.

Understanding the relationship between competitive position (through market share) and market growth is vital and several other techniques exist to help. Two of the most common examples are the Boston Consulting Group (BCG) growth–share matrix and the directional policy matrix, used and developed by GE and McKinsey (and sometimes called the GE-McKinsey model).

A question of emphasis

It should now be easy to decide where to invest your time – in other words, where to put the strategic emphasis. In general, there are six high-level options.

1 Grow the business – where you have good products and the market has growth potential.

2 Keep business levels steady – where your products are well established and reasonably successful, but perhaps the market is not growing significantly.

3 Reduce business levels – where your products serve this market less well, profit margins are low or other segments offer a better use of resources.

4 Stop selling this product to this market – where your products are not competitive or the market sector is not profitable.

5 Research new markets for existing products and new products for existing markets.

6 Diversify, launching new products into new markets (possibly through aquisition).

The figure below shows an example of strategic emphasis. In markets 1 and 2 for product 1, there is a strong competitive advantage and a decision has been made to maintain this. Market 3 provides an opportunity for growth. Product 2, on the other hand, is in a market that is not attractive and this is being de-emphasised for markets 1 and 2. Product 2 has no presence in market 3. Product 3 is a growth product and will be emphasised in all markets. However, some research needs to be done to validate whether product 3 would be successful in market 3.

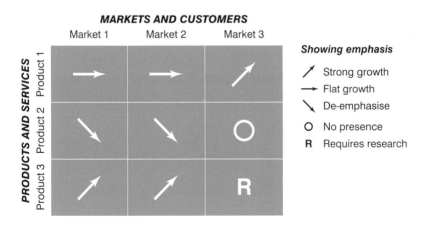

Describing the future scope of products and markets and choosing emphasis defines a key component of your business strategy. There are many strategic possiblities. At one extreme, some companies stay highly focused on their core market. They leverage this position by introducing new products into this market. Armani is a good example of a company driven by its position and expertise within the luxury goods market. Since its origins in designer clothing, it has extended its offering to include accessories and perfume, while staying true to its market and its customers. On the other hand, some companies are driven by the high-quality products they offer. They focus on the product but look for new markets to sell them to. A good example might be Toyota, a successful mass producer of cars that set up the luxury car subsidiary, Lexus, to extend its market at the high end.

6 EXTEND TO FUNCTIONAL DEPARTMENTS

In the planning process described so far, we have chosen markets and developed the necessary products to meet those market needs. This approach makes a lot of sense, but it is not the only one. Instead of starting with the customer, it is equally possible to think about what you are really good at internally as an organisation. These internal 'capabilities' can just as easily drive the strategic shape of the business. So while I have listed this as step 6 after the product marketing stage, there are many situations where the internal expertise is what drives which products are sold into which markets. If this is the case for your company, you might want to do this step first.

When trying to identify the competitive advantage of various capabilities or resources, ask yourself four questions using the VRIO[9] acronym:

1 Value – is there an opportunity to exploit this capability to deliver value (profit) for the organisation?

2 Rarity – is this capability or resource scarce (and likely to have a higher value)?

3 Imitability – is this capability or resource difficult (e.g. expensive or technically complex) to copy so that its advantages will endure?

4 Organisation – is the company well enough organised to take advantage of this resource or capability?

[9]Barney, Jay B. and Hesterly, William (2005), *Strategic Management and Competitive Advantage: Concepts and Cases*, Harlow: Pearson Education.

The capabilities discussed here may be so important that they become the key drivers of your strategy. Tregoe and Zimmerman[10] identified five (six if you include knowledge or expertise) capabilities that constitute what they called the 'driving force' of strategy. These six driving forces are manufacturing, method of sale, distribution, technology, expertise (e.g. management expertise for consultants or tax accounting expertise for audit firms) and natural resources. The driving force will be the most important part of the competitive advantage and will direct strategy – even though there are other 'secondary' capabilities that are needed to create an overall competitive advantage.

The table below gives example of companies which have excelled in developing internal capabilities that are the key drivers for their strategic success.

KEY CAPABILITY	EXAMPLES
Technology	Philips, Intel
Production capability	Corus, Richmond Ice Cream
Method of sale	Avon, Amazon, Boden
Distribution method	Virgin Media, UPS
Expertise	Capita, Accenture
Natural resources	De Beers, BP Exploration

In the examples here, it is the driving force that determines which products are sold into which markets. For example, Amazon started out as an online book retailer. However, it soon realised that its real competitive advantage was its method of sale, i.e. selling via the internet. Once established, it could extend product choice beyond just books, effectively selling anything that it could then deliver. It has of course extended its product line to include software, electronics and other goods. It would be reasonable to speculate that its driving force is the method of sale, although other capabilities are also very important. In particular, the high-quality distribution network is a 'secondary capability' that springs to mind as one that is vital to its success and overall competitive advantage.

[10]Tregoe, Benjamin B. and Zimmerman, John W. (1980) *Top Management Strategy*, New York: Simon & Schuster.

In the case of Intel, its ability to design leading-edge microprocessors became its driving force and hence it developed a strategy to identify different customers (typically PC manufacturers) who could embed this technology into their products. It could have decided that its competitive advantage was making finished products and used its chips to make computers, thereby preventing anyone else from using its proprietary technology. Think about what the core capabilities of your business might be and give special consideration as to how you might develop them. They are part of your competitive advantage and you need to continue investing in them.

Of course, not all capabilities will drive the future of the organisation, but they still require a carefully designed strategic plan. Even though distribution may not be a key capability, many companies still need to be competent at it. In fact, all functions or departments within the organisation need some sort of strategy to ensure that they support the higher-level priorities of the organisation. These subsets of the overall strategic plan are normally called functional plans. The following are typical areas of focus in the development of internal functional plans.

1 A sales and marketing plan aligned to the product marketing strategy.

2 An operational plan, looking at improving existing internal processes, such as customer care and account handling.

3 A technology strategy that allows improved operations in the future.

4 A human resource plan in alignment with other business strategies.

5 A sourcing plan that ensures a continued and competitive supply of raw materials, components or products that are strategic to your business, either for manufacture or on-selling; this might mean, for example, having a 'dual source' strategy for raw materials, typically from different countries.

6 A plan for strategic partnerships to help deliver capabilities that you cannot or don't want to provide.

For the majority of executives, their first strategy assignment is to assist in the development of one of these functional plans. It provides a perfect opportunity to develop strategic planning skills, as it is a strategy within a strategy. To be successful, it is very helpful to have the high-level strategic context as a guideline. It is quite common, however, for a functional plan to be developed without this. If there is a statement of mission or values, so much the better. In this case, it obviously makes sense to ensure that the functional plan fits within this. Nonetheless, all that is really needed is a clear understanding of the success measures of the function or department. These define the future goals, and from this the necessary projects can be identified. These high-level objectives may already be published or you may need to meet with senior stakeholders to firm them up. Either way, functional planning provides an excellent first opportunity to gain experience of strategic planning.

7 GENERATE A RISK REGISTER AND 'FUTURE-PROOF' THE PLAN

To ensure that your strategy is well thought through and will be able to withstand changes in business conditions, now is the time to look at different options and introduce flexibility into your plan. I recommend the following steps:

1 **After creating an initial strategy ask, 'Is there a better way?'** Examine different ways to achieve the business objectives, and choose the one that you feel has the best chance of success.

2 **Carry out a detailed risk assessment to understand the suitability of the strategy.** A corporate risk register should be maintained to monitor and manage key assumptions.

3 **Think of business conditions, both positive and negative, that would affect your business and assess how you might respond.** Although you will not be able to predict everything that will have an impact on your strategy, developing a series of the likely plausible scenarios will help the strategy to be more practical and resilient to changes in business conditions.

In my experience, you can develop high-level corporate objectives within a short time, often at the first high-level meeting. Many senior executives have preconceived ideas as to what the company will look like at the end of the strategic time frame (the period that the plan covers). This is not necessarily a bad thing, but it can be very helpful to challenge some of the basic assumptions. Targets are often ambitious and the supporting business unit plans usually have to overstretch to meet them. In step 7, take the chance to review the underlying assumptions of the core strategy and assess the risk of the supporting business unit plans.

The objective of this phase of strategic development is to find answers to the question, 'Is there a better way?' One of the best techniques for this is scenario planning. Scenario planning is a common management technique pioneered and used successfully in the 1970s by Shell. When applying it to your strategic process, you need to identify several plausible scenarios. Each scenario should provide an example of a possible, but perhaps slightly extreme, set of business conditions. The aim is to provoke a healthy discussion among the management team as to how the organisation would respond to each one. Scenarios should be both positive and negative.

On the negative side, you might ask what your response would be to a 30 per cent price reduction by the competition. Another scenario might look at the effect of disruptions to the supply chain or significant changes in client buying behaviour. First of all, the team needs to discuss how it would respond, and then secondly, how plausible it is that this scenario might take place. The outcome from scenario planning should include some preparation activities, allowing the organisation to respond quickly should that scenario come about.

On the positive side, you might review scenarios such as an increase of sales by 30 per cent, early launch of a particular new product or an innovative way of selling or distributing to clients. This stage in planning can sometimes bring to the surface significant new opportunities that were previously thought unattainable or were simply missed out. The high-level strategy can then be enhanced to incorporate these opportunities.

As the plans are brought together, you may find that some of the results of the strategic plan are in turn dependent on a number of key activities. In addition, new projects may emerge and it quickly becomes apparent that not all of them can be implemented safely within the time frame. Now is the time to identify key risks and document them in a central register. A typical risk register[11] from the functional strategic review of an IT organisation is shown in the figure below.

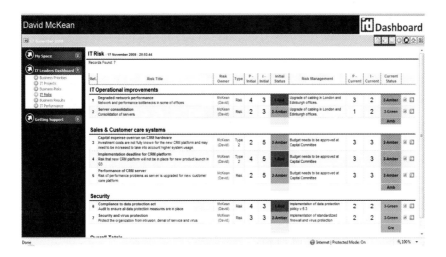

There are many different ways of calculating risk, but the most effective is to keep it simple. You need to consider two factors – how likely this risk is to happen in practice and then how serious it would be. To get a figure for how likely the risk is, consider its probability of happening in the strategic time frame and express this as a mark out of five. So if it is 40 per cent probable, score 2 and so on. Next, measure the severity, where 5 is catastrophic and 0 is no impact. Add the probability and the impact together to get an overall score – this should give a score out of 10 (very rarely it can be greater as, theoretically, the probability can be greater than 5, meaning that the risk will happen more than once in the time frame). Identify the top 20 or so risks and bring them together into the corporate risk register. Once the centralised register is in place, ensure that it is continually managed.

At the end of this stage, your strategy should be looking fairly robust, with a clearly defined product market matrix and a set of supporting business unit strategic plans.

[11]IT Leaders Ltd, 'Functional strategy and business alignment review: risk register'.

CASE STORY *FINANCIAL SERVICES, ROBINA'S STORY*

Narrator Robina worked for an international financial services company and was responsible for the sale of unit trust products to consumers. Within the broad strategic remit, she needed to look at several ways for reducing the cost of sale.

Context The board of directors of an international financial services company was concerned that the cost of sales to consumers of a range of unit trust products was too high.

Issue The main problem was that the sale of the current product portfolio required a lot of costly expertise for what was often a low-value outcome. Robina needed to take a strategic decision – either to sell only higher-level contracts or somehow to streamline the sales process.

Solution She took the decision to continue selling to domestic customers, whist recognising that the value of sale was unlikely to increase. This meant that the cost of sale had to be reduced. The first step was to simplify the financial product portfolio. The second step was then to improve the economics of selling. For this, the obvious option was to acquire the sales force from a competitor, on the basis that the economies of scale would significantly increase the profitability. This was only partially successful, though, and the board asked her to find an alternative.

At the time, the internet was gaining popularity, although it was unusual for financial products to be sold that way. The company devised a blended marketing strategy that combined good mail campaigns with clear product information on the web and financial advice when clients were close to making a final decision. The company was one of the first to successfully use the web for selling financial products.

Learning The company knew its market, and whilst it set clear and crisp objectives, it avoided imposing too many constraints. The requirement to reduce the cost of sale did not tie it to a particular solution. It is important in strategic planning to keep the focus on the outcome and look for different options to achieve it.

8 INTEGRATE ALL CORPORATE-WIDE PROJECTS AND KEY ACTIVITIES

So where are we now? The process started with an assessment of the current situation and then created a set of guidelines (identifying competitive advantage, basic beliefs and values) before identifying the future strategic goals. These goals described what you plan to achieve in all areas of the business – how to address customers and markets, how to improve internal capabilities, staff goals and financial results. You now need to put together the list of projects that will enable you to meet these targets. Some of these projects will already be under way and some new ones will need to be added.

Start by listing all your ongoing projects. It is often helpful to group these into similar categories, perhaps relating to the achievement of an individual goal. For example, if you are looking to increase sales in a new market requiring new products, updated information systems and additional sales staff, it can be helpful to group all these activities together. This reinforces the idea that meeting the end objective (increased sales in this case) is a team effort. The activities within each group need to be sequenced correctly – for example, only scheduling the new sales training when the product is ready for launch and the IT systems are fully working.

During the development of a strategic plan, a number of high-level corporate initiatives will be identified. These should be combined with ongoing projects to quantify the full scope of the change activity. The chances are that you will end up with a very long list of large and small projects, as well as individual tasks. Many companies make the mistake of adding new strategic initiatives to the existing project list. This can be disastrous as it has the effect of overloading the system, causing all projects to grind to a halt.

It is vital, then, that projects are prioritised. Only keep those that you have the resources to complete and defer or cancel the others. This review should be made and agreed by the whole team. You may find that some of the lower priority projects under way are quicker to finish than to stop. If you are asked to cancel projects, be sensitive as to how you handle the situation. It can be demotivating for team members to suddenly find their projects cancelled, particularly if they weren't involved in the decision. When the project list is clear, assign a sponsor to each one to ensure that they are completed and, more importantly, that the benefits are realised.

I am always amazed at how much more an organisation can achieve when it can visualise what needs to be done. It makes sense, therefore, to find a way of representing the plan on one page. The best way to start this is to summarise the key milestones from each of the main groups discussed in the previous paragraph. For each key group of projects, identify a number of key tasks or milestones. All project activity should be supporting a high-level goal. If this is not the case, you may want to ask whether the project should continue. Strategic planning often provides a good opportunity to drop projects that are no longer delivering the benefits expected.

QUICK TIP **CREATE THE HIGH-LEVEL PICTURE**
Create a high-level strategic view of key programme tasks and milestones. Print and laminate this chart on A3-sized paper and send it out to all employees.

Next, bring all the projects together and see how they match up to each other. Try to spread out the main deliverables over the whole year to avoid bottlenecks and the risk of spreading everyone's time too thinly. Look to sequence the key milestones evenly during the period. A milestone might be achieving a particular sales level, it could be the launch of a new product or it could be the go-live date of a new software application. Think about how to sequence these key tasks and milestones so that those delivering more benefit are done first. That way, even if things are delayed slightly, the maximum benefit will still be realised.

It can sometimes be helpful to map out the milestones on a large chart before they are formalised. Start by marking out the next two years on a large sheet of paper, say A2 or A1 size. Write each milestone on a Post-it note and place it where you think it should be complete. You can then decide which activities need to be moved up in order of priority and which ones can be delayed. Look to see if too many tasks are completing at the same time as this might suggest that there is a higher risk of

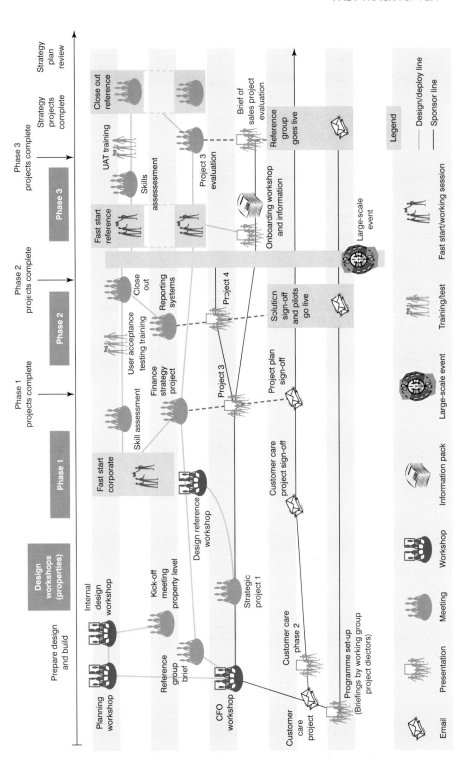

delay. For large multi-divisional organisations, this can be a complex task and may need a more formal approach with key members of the programme office working together to understand the global outline. Once you have this prototype chart, you can draw it up with one of the software tools such as Microsoft Project, Visio or PowerPoint. These are described in more detail in Chapter 4.

The figure on the previous page is an example of a strategic project plan drawn in a pictorial way. The individual tasks are joined together in the middle using a 'network diagram' format, with a summary timeline at the top. The tasks shown provide a good illustration of the shape and priorities of the overall plan.

9 ENGAGE AND EMPOWER THROUGH COMMUNICATION

The main activities for effectively communicating strategy are as follows.

1 Create a communications plan addressing the needs of shareholders, managers, employees and external partners.

2 Identify the most appropriate communication medium – for example, round table discussions, 'town hall' type presentations or one-to-one meetings.

3 Prepare the collateral materials for all presentations and communications.

4 Run the communications sessions for all stakeholders.

No two companies communicate in the same way, but in my experience the following four methods are the most common and most effective.

1 **A presentation of the high-level plan to all senior managers.** This can also act as a guiding script, so that all managers are consistent when presenting to the rest of the organisation.

2 **A 'town hall' type meeting to present the high-level strategy to the organisation.** The priorities here are to keep the presentation short, high level and motivational. One-to-one meetings may be

necessary if some employees are particularly affected by some aspects of the strategy. Remember that a new strategy will often require significant change for an organisation and its people. The management team should make sure that everyone not only understands what is going on, but also actively supports and embraces the change. Employees will quickly lose interest if all they hear is how the organisation will benefit. It is far better to show people what the benefits of change are for them.

3 **Smaller scale, more individually based presentations.** In some cases – for example where employees are working remotely or across international borders – it is more difficult for everyone to get together in the same place. In this situation, special consideration needs to be given to communication, for example via video link or face-to-face conferences.

4 **A document that describes the strategy in more detail.** The format of this document can vary. Many traditional companies, particularly professional services organisations, prefer that this is in a document or report format; others prefer a presentation format. Either way, it should be sent to the employees individually. You cannot expect that a document posted to the company intranet or internal website will be seen, let alone read, by all employees. Finally, update the company website with a statement of the 'external strategic messages' for clients and partners.

10 SUPERVISION OF PROGRESS

Senior management should monitor and review progress on a regular basis, to ensure the strategic plan is on track and delivering the required results.

1 Define the strategic objectives and link the personal objectives of all employees to them.

2 Have key stakeholders meet regularly to review the strategy and communicate the outcomes to the whole organisation.

3 Store all strategy related issues in a central location and use the regular stakeholder meetings to ensure they are resolved in a timely fashion.

4 Develop and implement an ongoing communications and governance structure, addressing the needs of shareholders, management, employees and partners.

Strategy is an ongoing process rather than something that happens once a year. The senior executive should meet once a quarter to discuss strategy and its progress. The strategic plan should incorporate all the major initiatives and subsequently measure their progress and the benefits they deliver. The following four aspects of the strategy plan should be considered at these meetings.

1 Tracking of major initiatives and realisation of benefits.

2 Testing of the initial assumptions that the strategy was based on.

3 Checking progress in terms of new products, new markets and diversification strategies.

4 Monitoring of the central risk register.

Furthermore, each employee should have a set of personal objectives that relate to the high-level corporate objectives. These should also be monitored and reviewed on a regular basis. Strategic objectives are defined in the four key quadrants of customer, process, people and finance.

All employees should have their personal objectives linked to the strategic scorecard, either directly or indirectly. A good example of a direct link might be in customer care, where the company wants to improve call waiting times. Each customer service representative would have their own call handling objectives. An example of an indirect objective might be the network engineer who is responsible for maintaining the routing of high traffic volumes to an outsourced call centre – delivering this successfully would also help call handling, but only indirectly.

STOP – THINK – ACT

After reading this chapter you will have learned about the different steps that the world's most successful companies follow to develop an effective strategy. Some will be more relevant than others to you, and some may need to be adapted to suit your specific situation. Take time now to reflect on the ten steps and summarise how you would use them to create a strategy relevant to your environment.

What should we do?	What tools and techniques are appropriate (one or two for each step)?
Who do we need to involve?	Who needs to be involved and why?
What resources will we require?	What information, facilities, materials, equipment or budget will be required?
What is the timing?	How long will each activity typically take?

Visit **www.Fast-Track-Me.com** to use the Fast Track online planning tool.

The challenges of leadership and strategy making in the third sector

Professsor David Birchall

EXPERT VOICE

As the third sector has grown in the UK over the last 10–20 years, new leadership opportunities have opened up for those suited to working in the not-for-profit enterprise. However, anyone considering a career move from a business enterprise should be aware that the leadership role requires a somewhat different knowledge base, certain forms of behaviour and a commitment to a different set of organisational values. At the same time, this sector is in need of the commercial approaches of business but in a way that is in line with the organisation's specific value set.

The third sector has grown due to the drive by governments to reduce the scale of the public sector, as well as the search for improved value for money in the provision of public services. It includes large charities such as Oxfam, with 7,000 employees in the UK, 22,000 volunteers in its shops and a turnover of £60m. Oxfam has a presence in 70 countries, even though many organisations are small and local in operation. In the main it depends upon public funding won in competition as well as donations from corporations and individuals.

The services provided by the third sector are wide ranging, but a recent survey[12] into just one segment, namely 'health and social care', estimated it comprised between 10,000 and 20,000 mid-sized organisations. Leaders responding to the survey were asked about the key challenges faced by their organisations. Much of their funding comes from fixed-term contracts, many of short duration. So for these executives the securing of funding is high on the agenda. The changing priorities of funding agencies, the constant squeeze on funding and its short-term nature make the formulation of a robust long-term strategy problematic. The organisations have to be responsive and flexible whilst still remaining true to the charity's goals. Often funding is awarded to partnerships rather than single providers. Sensitivity to the political environment, good use of strong networks, bid management and partnership building are the key leadership competencies.

Whereas business executives report to a board which has responsibility to shareholders, third sector organisations are answerable to a board of trustees. This body is likely to comprise a wide range of stakeholder interests. In many organisations in the third sector, the executive reports difficulties in working with trustees, feeling that it does not always get the strategic input sought, as well as actually lacking good governance and scrutiny due to lack of skills amongst trustees. This diverse group demands careful management attention.

Many third sector organisations depend upon a volunteer workforce. This renders inappropriate many human resources approaches used extensively in business to drive performance improvement. In addition, for those in employment, the salary levels generally do not compare favourably to those paid in business. Resources for training and development are constrained; in fact, resources in general are tight because funding agencies focus on spending money directly on delivery. So, all in all, the executive has challenges in strategy formulation and the development and management of an effective operation.

But for executives and managers seeking to move into the third sector there are clearly compensatory rewards. Much of this probably comes from the satisfaction of working in a social enterprise and providing services for the public good – a sense of making a real difference. Those who are successful in developing a sustainable organisation can feel justly proud of their achievement.

So strategy making in the third sector presents challenges not normally experienced in business enterprises, and for the leader a different style of management seems necessary for success.

[12]Stewart, J.A. and Birchall D.W. (2007), 'Looking after leaders – leadership development for leaders working in health and social care in the third sector', Henley-on-Thames: The Third Sector Leadership Centre.

TECHNOLOGIES

To remain as effective as possible, Fast Track managers differentiate themselves by the support mechanisms they put in place to help themselves and their team. These include the intelligent use of technology – enabling, for example, the automation of non-core activities, thereby freeing up time to focus on managing, motivating and leading people. They may also include the use of coaches and peer-to-peer networks, and gaining access to the latest thinking in their field.

Getting started

Why consider technology?

Technology plays a crucial role in the businesses of today and the work environment is barely recognisable compared to that of, say, 30 years ago. People take it for granted that they will have access to personal computers and other technology to do their jobs. Strategy development and technology have become inextricably linked. Although it cannot be completely automated, the careful use of good technology will certainly help you to foster good communication, enhance creativity and bring structure to your strategy. Choose your technologies carefully. Take care that your co-workers understand any tools and techniques you adopt and ensure that any information you use is accurate and relevant.

TOOLS (RED) TO SUPPORT THE STRATEGY PROCESS (BLUE)

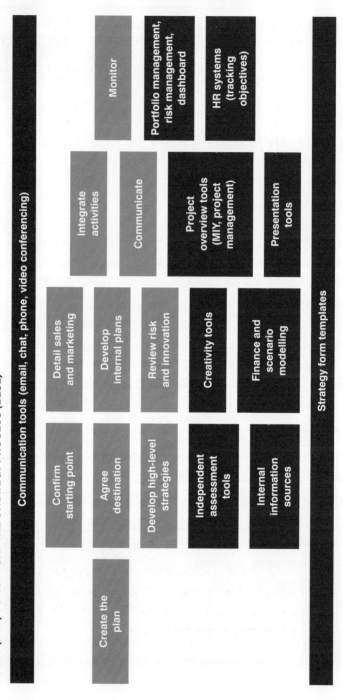

Communication tools (email, chat, phone, video conferencing)

Create the plan

Confirm starting point

Agree destination

Develop high-level strategies

Detail sales and marketing

Develop internal plans

Review risk and innovation

Integrate activities

Communicate

Monitor

Independent assessment tools

Internal information sources

Creativity tools

Finance and scenario modelling

Project overview tools (MIY, project management)

Presentation tools

Portfolio management, risk management, dashboard

HR systems (tracking objectives)

Strategy form templates

What should the technology do?

The chart opposite shows you where our selected technologies can help you in the strategic process. Think about which activities are complex enough or time consuming enough to warrant the investment in time and money. If you have been through the strategic planning cycle with your current organisation before, think about what worked and what didn't last time. Identify those areas which took up a disproportionate amount of time and see whether any of the tools suggested could help.

   Some technologies will be mandatory – for example, email and other communication tools. Others you may also have in place, such as project portfolio management or creativity software. Others may be new to you and you will need to think about the benefits they would deliver to your organisation. Much will depend on how large your company is and its willingness to invest. Many companies still think of strategy as an annual event and may be reluctant to invest in technology that is only used periodically.

Top technologies

How do I know what technology exists?

New technologies are coming on-stream all the time and successful managers in all disciplines need to keep up to date. Your biggest hurdle is often searching out the best solutions from the wealth of available information. This chapter gives you a start by identifying ten good technologies that will help you at different stages of developing your strategy.

What tools will support the development of strategy?

The following list provides a selection of technologies to investigate, but accept that it can be no more than a snapshot of what is happening at a point in time. Get into the habit of constantly scanning this field in search of new ideas for improving your strategic process.

1 Communication tools

What are they?   The success of your strategy will depend on how you communicate with your business colleagues. As a starting point most of your colleagues will be connected up with both phones and email, both in fixed locations and on the move.

If you are working with groups across international borders or even just separated by large distances, video conferencing can be a useful additional tool to help you to keep in touch. This technology has been around for a long time, but it is getting cheaper and better all the time. Audio and video information can now be transferred quickly enough over the internet. Voice information transferred in this way is known as Voice over Internet Protocol [VoIP]. Skype and MSN Messenger are examples of free-to-use VoIP and video conferencing systems that have been adopted by millions worldwide. These have the advantage of being cheap and easy to set up, and avoid the need to book expensive conference suites.

Many companies are implementing in-house instant messaging, using commercial versions of the MSN and Skype 'online chat' software. This allows people to keep in touch and carry on multiple conversations at the same time.

Pros   Email has the advantage that you can communicate with other people when they are not at their desks. It also provides an accurate record of conversations and helps provide a clear understanding. Emails can be easily copied to other participants anywhere in the organisation. Video conferencing has the advantage of being able to connect people in distant locations, not only hearing what they have to say but also seeing their faces, expressions and gestures. This will have the greatest impact on companies that have high levels of spending on international flights, but it can also reduce domestic travel costs. Instant messaging provides the same benefits as email with the addition of real-time response from a number of people at once.

Cons   It is easy for people to become overloaded with email. It can be reactive and involve too many people on less important discussions, particularly where there is a culture of 'cc-ing' (copying other individuals in on discussions). With email and instant messaging, there are (usually) no facial expressions or gestures, and the intent of the words can sometimes be misinterpreted. There is also the danger of it being seen as a substitute for face-to-face or phone communication. Video conferencing goes some way to eliminating those drawbacks but can be difficult and expensive to set up company-wide due to network costs.

Success factors   Use the technologies available to maintain regular communication with your business colleagues. Keep your messages simple and to the point, and make time to meet with your stakeholders and colleagues face to face on a regular basis.

QUICK TIP *USE TECHNOLOGY TO WORK STRATEGICALLY*

Look at the email replies you have sent out recently – say the last 200. Think about how you could respond more effectively or strategically in the future – and which ones you could avoid responding to altogether.

2 Strategic planning tools

What are they? Software tools are now available that allow you to capture key information in the development of your strategy. You define the format of a number of templates to capture the key information as your strategy is developed. This information can be stored centrally and you can amend the templates as your strategy process evolves. This allows the strategy project manager to see and monitor progress across the organisation. These strategy planning tools store information about the assumptions of the plan, key objectives, projects, risks and lessons learned. Project progress, risks and lessons learned can be tracked during the implementation of the strategic plans. If you don't have a central strategy planning tool, it is still important to capture the information in a structured way (using individual forms, tables and templates) and hold it centrally. Simple spreadsheet and database tools can often be adapted to meet the requirement, although they need more managing to keep them current and useful. Examples of these tools are available on the **www.Fast-Track-Me.com** website.

Pros Information is held centrally and in an agreed format for all stakeholders to review and update. It provides a way to evaluate previous plans and update them in the future, understanding what worked and what didn't. A well-designed tool allows you to capture the information that is relevant for your organisation and puts a structure around the process. Key documents (financial budgets, product plans, etc.) can easily be cross-compared against the strategic plan.

Cons These tools require an investment of time and money plus an understanding of the strategy process you wish to follow. There can also be a tendency to log only those ideas and insights that are positive, with less emphasis on learning from mistakes.

Success factors Develop a common view of the stages in your strategy development and the information you wish to capture. Keep the information current with regular reviews by senior stakeholders.

QUICK TIP *KEEP YOUR STRATEGIC FOCUS*
Book all four quarterly strategic review meetings at the beginning of the year. Your agenda should only include strategic issues for discussion, to avoid being sidetracked by operational problems. Bringing in outside facilitators can also help to develop new ideas.

3 Information sources to help with assessing your current position

3.1 The internet

As you look to identify your current situation, you will need to identify external, independent sources of information that will tell you how well you are doing relative to your competition.

The internet or World Wide Web is the first and usually most easily accessible source of information since it is based on global standards for sharing information. Most companies now allow internet access from work for employees.

Pros

The internet has the benefit of being free and major organisations all have their own websites. You can use it to get background information on your competition and a wide variety of relevant subjects in just a fraction of the time such research once took.

Cons

For reasons of confidentiality, companies won't put all information about themselves on their website – the customer references will be the best ones they have and the press releases will describe their current launches in positive tones. Be careful not to trust all information on the internet. Some of it can be out of date, and pages are rarely date stamped, so it can be difficult to tell. Given the amount of potentially distracting information, it is important to set yourself specific targets when searching to avoid the temptation of pointless 'surfing'.

Success factors

Use the web as a rich source of information and get into the habit of reviewing competitor and customer sites regularly. Take time to translate the large amounts of data from the web into usable information – for example translating information found on your competitors to an internal 'competitor database'. Finally, if new information is of critical importance then validate your conclusions using other sources. A neat rule of thumb is the one that journalists use – only publish a 'fact' if you have got at least two reliable sources.

3.2 Benchmarking

Benchmarking is the process of measuring yourself against the rest of the industry, usually using agreed metrics. Most industries have organisations that specialise in that industry and make it their business to know what is going on. The benchmarking organisation will either send you a questionnaire to complete and compare it with their database, or (for more money) assign one of their consultants to find the answers to their comparison questions.

Pros Benchmarking gives an organisation a good understanding of how it is performing relative to its competition. It provides hard facts and data to help a company to understand where it is performing well and which areas it needs to focus on – vital information for the development of good strategy. It can also provide useful insights into less tangible aspects of an industry, such as new product and customer trends, and the impact they might have in the future.

Cons Benchmarks can be expensive, even if you do the work yourself. There are also large differences in the performance of different companies in the same industry, and even though benchmarks are usually normalised for size and other factors, the complexity of cross-comparison can make it difficult to draw conclusions.

Success factors Make sure you choose a reputable benchmarking company with a good database of comparison data. Be clear what you want to benchmark and take time to understand any differences in the benchmark sample.

3.3 Customer surveys Customer surveys provide an opportunity to ask key customers a range of questions about the products they use today and how their priorities will change in the future. Surveys can be carried out over the phone, via email or in one-to-one meetings. You may also want to survey potential customers who are not currently using your products.

Pros Customer surveys provide a unique opportunity for you to talk to your customers in a positive way about how your products are used and perceived.

Cons If survey questions are not phrased carefully, you can get erroneous or misleading information back.

Success factors Design your questionnaire carefully and aim to survey customers every year. Select customers carefully but don't always ask the same ones. Treat your customers with care and respect during the process so that they know that their opinions are appreciated.

QUICK TIP KEEP ABREAST OF WHAT IS GOING ON
Get into the habit of taking ten minutes out each day simply to browse the internet. Get to know your customers, competitors and new technologies.

4 Internal sources of data – central knowledge management, management reporting and data warehouses

What are they? Internal sources of information are important to give you an insight into your operational performance and identify opportunities for improvement. They can include document management systems, internal management reporting systems and data warehouses. Document management systems such as SharePoint from Microsoft allow key information from the whole company to be managed and shared centrally, making co-working more efficient. Internal management reporting systems create performance reports using data from individual in-house operational systems such as financial, manufacturing or sales systems. Data warehouse systems are large repositories combining data from all operational systems to create more complex reports. Most data warehouses have online analytical processing (OLAP) tools which allow the data to be analysed easily in different ways. The data is held in what are called knowledge cubes and can be 'sliced and diced' in different ways.

Pros Having all the knowledge and operational information available centrally can provide the strategy team with vital information about past performance, including which products are profitable in which segments. Central document repositories often have valuable information about the market and competition. Management reporting tools provide the ability to quickly analyse data from different angles. This offers invaluable insights on the way products are used as well as possible future opportunities.

Cons Central document repositories can quickly get out of hand and become unmanageable. A bit like the internet, you can spend a lot of time looking through information that isn't relevant. Reporting systems in general and data warehouses in particular take time and sometimes major expense to implement. The data needs to be accurate to be usable and analysis of past results does not always provide accurate projections for future results.

Success factors Implement your reporting and data warehouse solutions by focusing on those areas where they will have most benefit. Analytical tools should be made available to those who need them, but try to foster an environment of cooperation so users do not recreate the same reports.

 CASE STORY **CABLE TELEVISION, JAN'S STORY**

Narrator Jan was the IT director for a major Dutch cable television and media company. He was responsible for building an IT functional plan to integrate with top-level business strategy.

Context Jan worked for a subsidiary of one of the world's largest cable companies based in the Netherlands. The company was embarking on a new strategic planning exercise to improve the efficiency of the internal processes, the performance of the network and the motivation of the staff.

Issue Jan had recently taken over as part of a new management team and was responsible for the information systems. IT has a particular role to play in all large organisations, and particularly in telecommunications, where customers are activated on to a live network. Jan's role was to provide an information technology plan that would support not only the high-level corporate objectives, but also the individual plans of the other departments, such as customer care, sales, HR and finance.

Solution The management team worked closely together to develop an integrated strategy. It was a top-down approach. The CEO set clear, ambitious and measurable high-level targets. More importantly, he gave guidance on the desired culture and behaviour and led by example. Jan took the high-level objectives and then worked with the individual functional managers. Between them, they identified a series of initiatives that would support the top priorities. By linking the plans together, they could see how the overall objectives were highly dependent on the joint working of the functional teams. Company turnover and profit figures changed dramatically over the following 18 months, as did the efficiency of processes, customer satisfaction and staff morale.

Learning All functional departments have two clear roles to play – they need to understand the high-level objectives as well as the individual objectives of the other functional teams. From this, they can develop their own plan that supports the other plans – known in IT as business alignment. This remains a two-way process, and once the plans are completed, they need to be checked against each other.

5 Tools for collecting and managing ideas and suggestions

5.1 Ideas pipeline The suggestion scheme is often the process for capturing new ideas and is open to contributions from all stakeholders. In contrast, those involved in the strategy process tend to use the ideas pipeline. An ideas pipeline is a database or spreadsheet that screens and prioritises ideas and enables Go/No-Go decisions to be made on a structured basis. Ideas should be ranked in order of priority, value to the organisation and the feasibility of a successful implementation. Ideas for the ideas pipeline should also be canvassed from an internal suggestion scheme.

Pros Once the pipeline is made visible to key stakeholders, it becomes an effective communication tool. Use of structured fields will dramatically improve the speed and quality of decision making at the regular review meetings (strategy board). Without a structured and visible approach, the wrong ideas are often selected based on personal bias or level of authority. The person organising the database can quickly detect overlap or competing ideas and resolve the issue to avoid wasting time and money.

Cons

If the list is allowed to become too big and cumbersome, it can be seen as bureaucratic, so it is vital that key stakeholders buy into the filtering criteria.

Success factors

Create a single database of ideas based around a structured screening and prioritisation process. Use it at monthly management meetings to drive decision making and kill off bad ideas quickly but sympathetically. Those who suggest ideas must be properly rewarded and have a say in how their ideas are put into practice.

Example

The web-based ideas pipeline below shows all the new market, process and product ideas generated by focused strategy workshops. Ideas have been assessed against impact and urgency, and a simple voting system using a star rating is used to set priority.

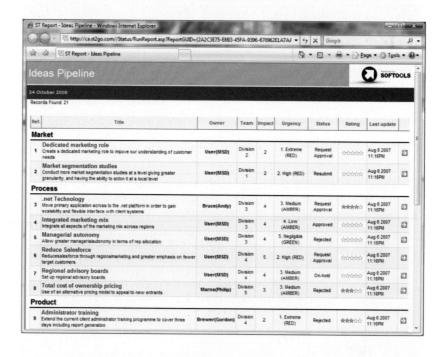

5.2 Creativity software	Software is becoming increasingly flexible and capable of stimulating creative thought – either for individuals working on their own or for groups in a brainstorming session. Products offer graphical or structured ways of generating and developing new ideas beyond the initial concepts. An example would be a 'mind-mapping' software application that allows you to link ideas in a pictorial format.
Pros	It appeals to people that think in pictures and those that need graphics of concepts in order to bring them to life. Used effectively, it will increase levels of challenge and creativity.
Cons	Many people don't like graphical representation of ideas and can find them confusing – much as some people find maps easy and intuitive whilst others don't.
	Most teams use standard applications such as spreadsheets or databases shared across the intranet to monitor and control new ideas during implementation. Whilst mapping software can be very creative, the ideas are often not that easily transferred to standard desktop or web applications.
Success factors	Explore alternative software packages that offer mind-mapping and creative idea generation options, but don't commit unless you are sure they are better than good old Post-it® notes.
Example	The mind map on the next page shows the high-level structure of a training company's strategy. The graphical format enabled them to draw links between the items and to fundamentally change the top level structure.

6 Budget and scenario management tools

What are they?	Your strategy will ultimately be driven by objectives and targets, and hence it will have a strong financial component. Top organisations want to see how changes in one part of a strategy impact another – for example, working out the effect of increasing the sales force on the number of new products sold, support calls, revenue and margin. Being able to simulate the business conditions and quantifying the effect of different business drivers is essential for good strategic planning.
	Spreadsheets are the main simulation and budgeting tool for most organisations. Key input variables such as competition levels, projected sales and pricing are entered. The output results can then be calculated. Results are not just financial results such as revenue and profitability. They could include anything from service quality to asset utilisation. In the case of the hotel industry, this would include occupancy rates, whilst for telecommunications companies it would be network capacity, and so on.

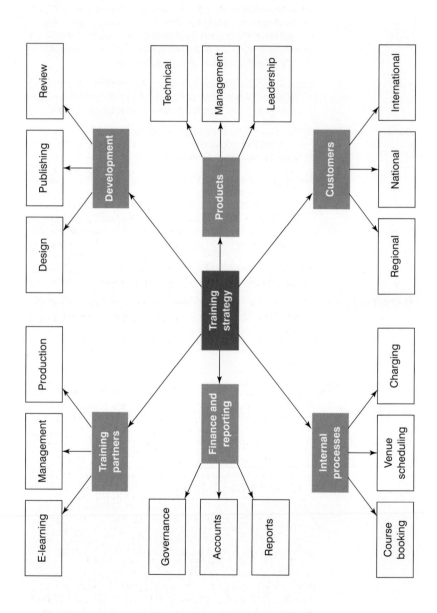

Once a budget has been prepared, it is important to understand whether the strategic plan is resilient to changes in business conditions. Look to identify several (five or so) different business scenarios and see what impact each has on your key results. Typical scenarios might include the impact on your plan if one of your main competitors is acquired by another, or the implications of an economic downturn.

This type of analysis will identify areas of vulnerability. You may find, for example, that a decrease in sales of a highly profitable product inhibits development of a new product, which in turn has a knock-on impact on the whole plan.

Pros   Spreadsheets enable organisations to analyse large-scale and complex information and are particularly suited to financial projections. They allow different variables to be modelled quickly and accurately.

Cons   Analysing historical information and making projections for the future can be dangerous, often leading to overambitious targets. Such scenarios can become too complex over time as new variables are added year on year, making them prone to errors. They are usually owned by the finance department, and often one expert within that department. This creates the risk that they can't be properly verified and are vulnerable if that person leaves the company.

Success factors Rein in the complexity of spreadsheets and ensure they are driven by the strategic thinking of senior management – not the other way round.

7 Tools for visualising the plan

What are they? When you are creating your strategic plan you will want to bring it to life and the best way to do this is to show it pictorially. Several tools exist that can help with this. MakeItYours is an example of a low-cost tool that was developed specifically for creating paths to success and has been used for individual goal setting as well as for companies worldwide. It lets you picture the progress of key strategic initiatives, with icons marking key progress points on the way. Other more generic project and presentation tools (such as Microsoft PowerPoint, Visio or Project) can also be used.

Pros   Putting a strategic plan into pictures will help the team to really see what the future will look like and how they will get there. It needs to be specific enough to be useful but also stimulating enough to capture attention and inspire. I have seen project management tools used effectively to create a visual representation of a plan. It is important to do this using the network format (sometimes referred to as a PERT chart) and not the timeline format (also known as a Gantt chart). Arrange the tasks carefully in groups so everyone can see which tasks go together and how the plan looks at a high level.

Cons   It can take time to produce this, although in my opinion it is a mandatory part of strategy. Some investment in the necessary tools may be needed.

Success factors Your representation should be an accurate view of the strategy and be specific enough to be of value. Invest an appropriate amount of time and money to create your 'picture'.

8 Tools to help the audience understand the strategy

What are they? When your plan has been created, you will need to develop communications materials to help you share your vision with different groups using different media. The strongest way to get your messages across it usually via a presentation. There are many presentation software packages but the best known is Microsoft PowerPoint. Make your presentation interesting and informative, with a good use of pictures, charts, drawings and models and keep the words per slide to a minimum. Aim for no more than 12 slides and ideally fewer.

You can also make your presentation much more interesting by adding animation or video. It can provide a fast and entertaining way to introduce new employees to an organisation. Once you have communicated your message, you may wish to add your presentation to the intranet as a reminder for your audience.

Pros A well-crafted presentation will make a lasting impact on your audience, leaving them not only better informed but also inspired to take on the challenge.

Cons Over time, but often unnoticed, some organisations develop a culture of long and detailed presentations. This is not only time consuming but also difficult for an audience to absorb. Short presentations are much better.

Success factors Plan what you are going to include in the presentation at the beginning and don't keep adding to it. Concentrate on making the slides interesting and informative. Keep your presentation informal and allow plenty of time for questions.

9 HR and payroll systems – linking strategic objectives with personal performance

What are they? Every company needs a payroll system of some kind and most payroll software applications have a human resources (HR) module that captures information on employees' performance and development. It is very important for employees to understand how they contribute to the strategic goals. These contributions should be set out as objectives that form part of the employee's performance appraisal. HR systems allow these objectives to be properly recorded and tracked and can be used as the trigger for bonus payments.

Pros Most payroll packages have HR modules which can be added, allowing the central management of objectives.

Cons HR modules can be overkill for small organisations.

Success factors If you are implementing an HR module, keep it simple and only use it for applications that have clear benefits.

10 Tools for project portfolio and risk management – monitoring the success of strategy

What are they?	Once you have developed your strategy, you will want some governance tools in place to monitor progress. There are a number of tools available for monitoring operational and strategic performance. Often your financial and manufacturing systems will monitor your operational key performance indicators (KPIs), but you also need to monitor strategy change.
	In the last few years, portfolio management tools have become a common tool for monitoring the status and success of change programmes. The tool captures common information from the project process and centrally monitors the status of all projects.
	It is also possible to set up a risk register, allowing the strategy governance process to actively monitor corporate risk. The progress of strategy and operational results can be summarised in a digital dashboard.
Pros	If set up correctly, these tools provide a company-wide view of all business and technology projects under way in the organisation. They allow better project prioritisation and create a culture of continuous improvement as project benefits are more accurately measured.
Cons	They require an investment in money and agreement for a standard project and risk process.
Success factors	Quickly agree your standard project and risk processes and make them simple enough for the whole organisation (traditionally, IT organisations have driven project management processes and as a result they can be complex).

QUICK TIP **LEARN FROM THE PAST**

Think through some of the technologies and techniques that you have used in previous organisations and identify which of them would add value to your current organisation.

How do I keep balance?

Now stop. Before going out and investing in the latest and greatest, remember that technology is just an enabler. Success will ultimately depend on your ability to lead others, your interaction with them and your behaviour.

Be wary of being drawn into new technologies too quickly – let someone else make the mistakes, but then learn quickly. Finally, if you do decide to introduce new systems into your team, think carefully about the possible risks – in other words, what could go wrong?

STOP – THINK – ACT

You may already have been aware of many of these modern technologies; however, you should now understand how each can be used to support the adoption of a common approach to strategy based on the best practices. Use technology selectively to drive performance in ways that minimise complexity, bureaucracy and cost.

Reflect on each of the technologies presented and ask yourself and the team these questions:

What should we do?	What technologies are available that will help to improve effectiveness and efficiency?
Who do we need to involve?	Who would benefit and why?
What resources will we require?	What level of investment would be required?
What is the timing?	When would be a good time to introduce the new technology – is there a 'window of opportunity'?

Visit www.Fast-Track-Me.com to use the Fast Track online planning tool.

Working with your coach[1]
Dr Laurence S. Lyons

As a modern business leader, it is likely that at some stage in your career you will find yourself working with an executive coach. Any good coach will deliver immense value to both the Fast Track leader and the organisation for which they work. But how do you define your coach's role, how should you select your coach – if indeed you find yourself fortunate enough to have such a choice – and how will you go about measuring benefit along the way?

[1]Goldsmith, Marshall and Lyons, Laurence S. (2005), *Coaching for Leadership, The Practice of Coaching from the World's Greatest Coaches*, San Francisco: Wiley-Pfeiffer

EXPERT VOICE

Ask these questions and you enter a minefield. These days, everyone's become a coach. Should you find yourself working with someone who isn't right for you, the main dangers are wasting your time and missing opportunities. If you can choose, then choose with care.

Naturally, you are more likely to maximise the value from your coaching experience by taking a strategic approach. But being aware of your career stage and situational context are equally important. That's because, by its very nature, you should expect your coaching adventure to uncover new insights and possibilities. By all means set out on your journey as would any manager – planning to achieve your desired outcome. But if you want to develop as a leader, be prepared to review and refine *what that outcome might be* as you travel along your way. Such is the art of informed strategy.

Given that you've found someone who is presentable and trustworthy, one way to recognise a good coach is through professional membership of a reputable body. This is perhaps most applicable to the programme coach who generally works to some predefined format or is trained to use a particular assessment instrument. Alternatively, a coach is distinguished by personal brand. This is more appropriate where the scope of work is less well defined and a coach becomes known through achievement and reputation. Here are some typical coaching situations.

→ **The expert coach.** In the same way that an expert consultant refreshes your *knowledge*, the expert coach is adept in helping you develop your *skills*. An expert coach may bring out your talents in public speaking, get you writing better management reports, help you improve your time management, get you chairing meetings more professionally and so forth.

→ **The programme coach.** Increasing numbers of forward-thinking organisations are realising the need for middle manager development stretching beyond simple off-site training. Corporate leadership programmes, often employing a *360-degree feedback system*, have maximum impact when personally interpreted by a programme coach who can help translate the harvested data into action on the ground. Some programmes include psychological assessments such as Myers Briggs Type Indicator (MBTI) and Hogan Personality Inventory (HPI),[2] and the coach working on such programmes should have specialist experience in deploying these in a business context. Just as important is the coach's role in follow-through; coaching is a programme, not an event.

[2] MBTI and HPI are proprietary assessment tools. All trade marks acknowledged.

→ **The senior or C-level coach.** This kind of coach is most effective when working without an agenda. Life gets turbulent at the CEO, CFO, COO level and your coach needs to be sufficiently nimble to go with the flow. This coach is more likely to bring a depth of personal experience, having worked at a strategic level either as a seasoned executive or polished staffer. In addition to strategy formulation, proficiency in change management and organisational politics are essential. C-level coaches are likely to be recognised by reputation ,as their ability to fit comfortably into the mundane programme role would almost certainly disqualify them from doing their job.

A debate rages as to whether coaches should be measured on return on investment (ROI) or value for money (VFM), criteria. Perhaps surprisingly the question of metrics is most easily dealt with at the C-level. Senior executives know when they are getting value from their coaching sessions and, equally, when they are not. If there's ever any doubt, maybe it's time to stop.

IMPLEMENTING CHANGE

Planning the way ahead

Managing change is difficult for any company, but when you create a strategy, you will have to do it not once but twice – first when you create the strategy and secondly when you implement it (see figure below).

The first cycle of change starts when the strategic planning process kicks off and ends when it is communicated to the organisation. If your organisation has a culture of strategic planning, this cycle will be straightforward. If not, you may well encounter serious resistance, so it is important to understand the process and to be prepared.

The second cycle starts when your strategy is first announced and (in theory) ends when its change programmes are implemented. Of course,

STRATEGIC PLANNING CYCLE	BUSINESS IMPLEMENTATION CYCLE
Strategic planning change issues	**Business implementation change issues**
• Changes to the way strategy planning is done	• Changes not communicated properly
• Decisions affecting the way things are done	• Staff not agreeing to the strategic changes proposed
• Fundamental differences of opinion	• Responsibility not handed down to the affected team
• Handling proposals for changing responsibilities	• Change projects not delivering early benefits
	• Changes not followed through

in practice, most successful organisations are constantly changing and hence the implementation of change programmes will never end. For this reason, strategic change projects are often best implemented in phases, each with clearly identified benefits. There is nothing more certain to stop a project than long periods of struggle with nothing to show. Your role is to stay close to the 'main projects' and make sure that they are completed. The main projects will be the ones that deliver the most business benefit and will probably have the greatest impact on your staff and customers.

As you follow the project plan and create your 'hard' deliverables, such as the market analysis work, scenario calculations and so on, you will also need to consider the human impact. Assessing performance, developing innovative ways of improving results and implementing plans affect both the work that employees do and the way they do it. These are the subjective or emotional aspects of strategy. They need careful handling or they may prevent a successful outcome.

As you look ahead, you may already be able to see some of the problems. At your first planning meeting, you may wish to ask the team what obstacles they envisage too, based on previous years' experiences. Typical problems include people not adopting the proposed changes or only the parts they were interested in. In my experience, you will get a lot of suggestions that highlight the fact that this is an exercise in emotional change as well as objective business change. Again, handling the emotional aspects of the strategic planning process is a serious issue and must be done sensitively.

Emotional conflicts tend to have one of two root causes. In the first situation, a strategic change is needed but it has a negative impact on the work life of an employee or group of employees. If you are running a team and this happens to your people, you will need to spend time with those affected to help them understand the need for the change. Work with them to agree a 'win-win' outcome in the new world. A good example of this may be closing an office which is only partly used. Employees may resist this because it is near to their home and the alternative means a long commute. Different solutions can be put forward, such as allowing staff to work more from home, renting a smaller office or even offering special severance terms. Strategy can often mean making difficult decisions and they need to be approached with a strong resolve.

But it helps no one in the long term to sustain a situation that makes no commercial sense.

The second root cause of emotional conflicts is where two parties fundamentally disagree about what the right strategic course might be. An example might be deciding the right time to diversify into a new market, make an acquisition or close a factory. Of course, no one will ever know the right answer. The best you can do is to make the choice – to diversify or not diversify, to acquire a company or not, or to close the factory or leave it open – based on rational decision making. You will only ever know whether the option that you chose works out – you will never know how the options you didn't choose might have fared. Early on in your strategy career you may not be involved in these core discussions – and sometimes it is politically expedient to stay clear. But as you progress, you may have to intervene. Try to keep the decisions fact-based and give the team every opportunity to discuss matters in a professional and objective manner.

However good your initial predictions, you will no doubt encounter further unexpected problems. Problems occur at different stages of the process and can affect the motivation of the workforce. For example:

→ **The annual business forecasting process becomes disconnected from the long-term priorities of the strategic plan.** The problem is compounded by the fact that this annual process is used to set departmental budgets as well as employee bonuses. A common example is sales force commissions. If the product market mix is changed as part of the strategy, sales targets can be out of line with strategic goals.

→ **The people who set strategy do not possess the detailed knowledge and are unaffected by the proposed strategic changes.** This causes resentment and a lack of 'buy-in'.

→ **When analysing the current situation, there is insufficient data upon which to make a decision.** This is often evident when trying to understand the competitive market forces. Major strategic decisions end up being based on a range of risky assumptions and people lose confidence in what they are trying to achieve.

→ **Even though the strategy is well communicated, the management team become disconnected from the rest of the organisation.** Management lose credibility and support when they do not 'walk the walk'.

→ **Executives meet regularly to discuss strategy, but get sidetracked into resolving short-term issues and end up changing strategic decisions for tactical reasons.** People lose faith in the process because changes don't stick and they return to their normal way of working.

The point here is that we are not dealing with a mechanical process but with people. Unless you have been through a similar strategic process before, you will not be able to predict where these problems lie. To be successful you will need to:

→ set up a high-calibre team and maximise their potential to succeed;

→ create an effective implementation plan with achievable milestones;

→ manage the process as a business change initiative;

→ provide leadership through the process.

How should we introduce change?

Science has shown that too much change literally does make people feel uncomfortable. This relates back to our primeval instincts and the 'fight or flight' response. When we cannot rationalise what we see in front of us or what we are being asked to do, our instinct is to fight or take flight. In the workplace, this manifests itself in many different ways. Some people react by ignoring any proposed changes and continuing as though nothing had happened, hoping it will go away – the 'flight' response. Some choose to 'fight' and react by disrupting the proposed changes.

However, there is some good news. It is believed that the human brain rewards us for coming to terms with new challenges, giving us a sense of increased knowledge, security and, in turn, well-being. So, as long as the initial onslaught is not too great and similar changes have been rewarded in the past, our instincts encourage us to try new things. It is quite common, though, to see managers who are unaffected by a change to be enthusiastic, whereas those affected are not. In this case, we have two distinct groups of people, each coping with a very different level of change, although crucially the company only recognises one. This is a warning sign, because those who are more deeply affected often understand the implications more fully.

In this case, it is important to ensure that those most affected by the change have some say in how that change is implemented. This is particularly good news as it means that plans should not be too detailed, but rather describe things in general (but clear) terms and let those most affected work through the details.

QUICK TIP **QUICK WINS FOR STRATEGIC PROJECTS**
Look through your current strategic project portfolio and check that all the projects have 'quick win' deliverables.

Ensuring success – keeping the plan on track

What routines should we set up?

Developing strategy is one of the most important roles of senior management. But given that most senior managers are extremely busy in day-to-day activities, status updates should be kept to a minimum.

Usually you will have one key sponsor, typically a senior director or the managing director. Arrange a weekly meeting and try to keep it to just half an hour. If your progress update is clear, it may only take a few minutes to present. Use the remaining time to address the high-level issues. Don't feel obliged to use your whole time allocation. Senior managers will thank you for taking less time than allocated – and they will then be more willing to allow you ad hoc time when you need it.

Every two to three weeks, you will want to bring the whole team together to align the different project streams. Put together a clear agenda with specific deliverables to maintain the sense of urgency. Remember to set the date and time for the next meeting before ending the current one.

Your weekly routine should also include a one-to-one catch-up with each of the other key stakeholders as well as the individual project members. Keep these meetings short and to the point, with the aim of maintaining project momentum in between the main team meetings.

With most projects you can extend the project completion date to include additional key functionality, but this does not apply with developing strategy. With strategy you will more likely have an immovable deadline – usually the annual planning cycle. Delaying beyond this date is not an option for two reasons. Firstly, your strategy will be a key driver for budgets which are set at this time. Secondly, it will determine the high-level and individual objectives for the organisation, which may in turn be linked to salaries and bonuses.

This will put pressure on you. Your first reaction may be just to start earlier, but this can also be dangerous. The organisation will not have the necessary sense of urgency if it believes there is a lot of contingency in the plan. The reality is that you will only be allowed a small margin for error in your plan. If you are working as the project lead on strategy, your role will be to ensure that all milestones are reached. You will have to carefully balance the time available on each of the phases. You don't want to spend all your time 'analysing the current situation' and then find that you have no time to draw up an integrated high-level plan or to communicate the strategy to the organisation. Be careful how you allocate time to the plan and be prepared to act early to move on to the next stage of the process.

 CASE STORY *LOCAL GOVERNMENT, PETER'S STORY*

Narrator Peter was head of customer operations, looking to implement a major strategic change programme to improve first-time call resolution. His story highlights the importance of good communication in all aspects of strategy and business change.

Context A city council was looking to upgrade the customer care systems as part of a strategic initiative to provide better information to residents and Peter was asked to run the project. The new system would simplify some operations and make it easier for customer service representatives (CSRs) to handle a wider range of questions.

Issue The upgrade had suffered some early delays and this had led to a loss of confidence in the project. Peter brought in a new technical team who, after an intensive period of work, got the project back on schedule. With one month to go-live, Peter received a petition signed by over 100 CSRs asking that the upgrade be delayed. It transpired that with the early project delays and the arrival of the new technical team, the customer care team never expected the project to be completed.

Solution Although the customer care team had not been engaged on the project for some months, the functionality of the new system had not changed. A programme of training was put in place to bring the CSRs up to speed, and when this was complete, the system successfully went live – six weeks later than planned.

Learning Managing change is a constant priority for all strategic projects. All employees affected by the change need to have a say in how things turn out and be regularly updated. Above all, they need to see progress and believe that the change will be beneficial.

How do we stay flexible?

Having your routines in place, including regular meetings with your key sponsors, one-to-one meetings with the other key team members and a project plan that maps out the key stages, will give you a good foundation for success. Inevitably, though, you will encounter problems in the development of your strategy and you will need enough flexibility in your routines to resolve them. A former Special Forces boss of mine used to tell me that 'indecision is the key to flexibility'. In other words, don't rush to make a decision if you don't have to, as it will restrict your options later on. It is easier not to make a decision than to make it and then have to reverse it. Don't try to predict every aspect of the work ahead while you are still in the early stages of planning – the most common mistake is creating a long list of tasks, causing the project to fall behind early on and lose momentum.

QUICK TIP CHOOSE A STRATEGIC TEAM
Think about adding strategic and creative thinking to your selection criteria when recruiting people to join your team and look for a balance of skills and personalities.

Flexibility in planning is also important. An example might be the sign-off of high-level objectives. Perhaps the team put together a list of high-level objectives but disagreed on the targets for a couple of them. An inflexible planning process might prevent the functional teams from starting to develop their own plans until all high-level objectives were agreed. It makes more sense in this case to move on to the next phase, but to agree the final objectives at the earliest opportunity.

To give yourself flexibility, give some thought to the type of issues you may encounter. It is easier to switch to a different option if you have done some pre-planning. The most common problems relate to the availability of team members. Sometimes they get moved on to other urgent projects or transfer to different parts of the organisation. The problem of availability is most prevalent with senior executives and you will often need to have your options ready in advance. Think about the other problems you are likely to encounter on your project and develop contingencies to avoid them causing delay.

In summary, when planning the strategy process, keep the project plan at a high level so you have flexibility in how long it takes to complete the overall task, but include enough detail to be able to see regular progress. Aim to include no more than 20 tasks in your outline plan and keep project dependencies to a minimum.

Critical success factors

So how can we increase our chances of success?

There are no real secrets in the development and implementation of strategy. Nonetheless, those companies that are particularly successful tend to use the following guidelines.

Don't over-plan

Having a good plan with the right amount of detail and a practical routine of meetings is the first stage to success. If this is the first time that different members of your team have worked closely together to develop a joint strategy, you will need to take this into consideration, making sure that everyone understands the process and their role in it.

Get the tools in place early

By now you will have identified tools that will help you develop your plan and communicate as a team. These might include the templates required for capturing information on your current situation, risks and suchlike. It might include setting up central document sharing folders or access to particular management reporting systems. Endeavour to have all these tools up and running before the project starts and ensure that everyone knows how to access and use them.

Handle conflicts early

Strategy is a tough puzzle to solve. The team will be stretched in their thinking and have pressures on their time. They will be looking at procedural changes, organisational changes and cultural changes. This pressure will often give rise to conflict. As a leader in your organisation you will need to identify and resolve these issues quickly if the project is to be a success. Often face-to-face discussion is all that is needed, but in some cases you will need to change team members. The key is to act decisively and so prevent other team members from losing momentum.

Don't do too much

Perversely, one of the best ways you can increase your chances of success is to do less. Don't write long and detailed documents. Keep your deliverables simple and concise. Avoid vague summaries and ensure your strategy is based on facts and data wherever possible. When it comes to implementing the strategy itself, limit the number of strategies and changes being followed at any one time.

Focus on the priorities

Focus on those aspects of the strategy that will deliver the best results. When you do your product/market segmentation, you will find that most of your revenues and profits come from a few of those segments. Often the 80/20 rule applies, and if it does, focus on those segments that produce the 80 per cent of the result. The French have a saying that 'perfection is the enemy of the good'. This holds true with strategy, where spending too much time trying to get to the 'right answer' becomes counter-productive as it delays completion and disrupts the plan.

QUICK TIP *STOP ANNOYING YOUR CUSTOMERS*
Think about those things that your customers find most annoying (or better still, ask them) and work out how you would fix them, first of all with unlimited resources and then with limited resources.

Consider the workload of team members

Don't forget to consider your team members and recognise that most of them will have other work to do. If you have templates that need completing, tailor them for each group. Don't ask them for information that does not apply to their domain of responsibility. Templates should follow the principles of project plans – make them specific enough to capture the right information but not too detailed that they become a chore.

Ensure enough resources

A strategy team may be drawn from different departments and different locations and have different priorities. It is important that you keep everyone's attention focused on the project. Get clear commitments from all the key players that they will devote enough time to complete their deliverables. If you require other resources, such as office space and budget, these should also be agreed at the beginning of the project.

Don't be too soft

Running a strategic planning project with a virtual team can sometimes feel a bit like herding frogs. Every time you think you have rounded up and completed an issue, another one pops up. And while you try to solve that, the first one reappears. This sort of problem is typical when people are balancing different priorities. It is tempting to accept delays as inevitable. This is dangerous. When team members ask for a delay or cannot make commitments, they should be held to account. Sometimes you will need a firm hand to get the job done.

Communicate success

Finally, communicate successes or 'quick wins' to all stakeholders so that people can see that the overall approach is working and worthwhile.

STOP – THINK – ACT
After reading this chapter you will be aware that implementing a comprehensive approach to strategy is not necessarily quick or easy. You will encounter problems during the creation and implementation stages. For this reason, change needs to be planned and implemented using a disciplined approach. Think about the effect that the strategy review is having on people around you and what problems it might be causing.

What should we do?	What stages and tasks are appropriate?
Who do we need to involve?	Who needs to be involved and why?
What resources will we require?	What information, facilities, materials, equipment or budget will be required?
What is the timing?	How long will each activity typically take?

Visit **www.Fast-Track-Me.com** to use the Fast Track online planning tool

Practical strategy

Dr Laurence S. Lyons

What kind of strategist are you?

Whether your business is an adventurous start-up, an effervescent trail-blazer or finds itself drifting aimlessly into serene obscurity, strategy is important for its survival. Similarly, as an executive, your ability to think strategically is perhaps the most essential skill you need to promote your career growth. Executives who neglect putting the necessary work into honing their strategic skills are in serious danger of derailment.

As a Fast Track executive, it is likely that you will have already formed an opinion about strategic thinking. If you are highly task oriented you may take the view that all strategic activities are a complete waste of time. If you're strongly driven or highly intuitive, you may think that your strategy is so blindingly obvious that it's hardly worth taking the time to explain it to others. Perhaps you just don't have the patience to deal with strategy but prefer to get your head down and get on with the job in hand.

Then again, you may be strategy's strongest advocate and biggest fan – investing endless hours running blue-sky meetings or analysing reams of data which give pinpoint accuracy of what happened in the distant past, while no actual productive work gets done. Without a doubt, many of the activities carried out in the name of strategy justifiably deserve harsh criticism. And it's also true that strategy has been given a bad name by its unfair association with the meaningless jargon of 'management speak'.

But it's also the case that many brilliant proposals – perhaps the very best ideas – come to nothing. That's often because the genius who had that great idea failed to express it in a way which allowed senior management and funding sources to understand and fully support it. The successful executive not only has to be smart but must inspire others by communicating to them in the purposeful language of business: that language is strategy.

Although its name suggests that it's mainly a cerebral activity, the really difficult part of strategy lies in its implementation. Those rare people who properly implement a good strategy consistently succeed. So what elements make up a good strategy?

In the leadership context, strategy traditionally boils down to three fundamental questions for the business:

1 Where are we today?

2 Where do we want to be tomorrow?

3 How do we get there?

At business conferences over the past 15 years I've frequently asked groups of leaders this simple question: of the three questions of strategy, which one do you consider is the most important? In other words, if you could know with certainty the answer to only one of these three questions, which one would that be?

The results are always broadly the same. Of those who feel confident to answer (that is the vast majority), approximately one-half vote for the first question. Typically, these are the leaders who feel comfortable only when they have a stack of large reports piled high on their desks. If they could be given an extra minute to polish their planning, they'd spend every second collecting more data. These leaders are in danger of *paralysis by analysis*. Knowing with total accuracy where the business stands today will not help one jot in moving it forward into the future.

Just under half the leaders want to know where they'd like to be tomorrow. These are the visionaries. They love drawing the big picture; they insist on including all manner of political, economic and social trends and pay great homage to the revered scenario. But by itself, insight into the future cannot offer practical advice in helping business leaders know what they have to *do* differently right now.

In my experience, roughly three leaders in a hundred vote for the third option, but this is the only question which forces a practical answer. If we know what *action* we must take, that our plan is feasible and that we have the collective determination to succeed, surely we will be in need of nothing. Yet only a tiny minority of leaders acknowledge this. Where did you cast your vote?

Of course, life is never this simple and perfect knowledge in business is an unattainable ideal. But a seasoned leader knows how to put up with imperfection. The successful leader sees strategy as a disciplined way of thinking, as a language, as a means of enlisting support and as a practical tool which helps the business make progress.

The past and the future cannot by themselves suggest policy. Their strategic role, however, is to inform it. The ability to think both strategically and practically at the same time is the hallmark of a successful leader. How you decide you will think about strategy is a key to your success.

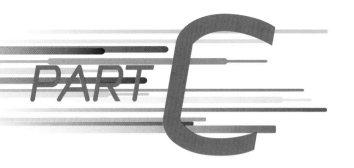

CAREER
FAST TRACK

Whatever your management career, to be successful you need to take control, plan ahead and focus on the things that will really make a difference.

The first ten weeks of a new role will be critical. Get them right and you will be off to a flying start. Get them wrong and you will come under pressure and even risk being moved on. Plan this initial period so that you are not overwhelmed by the inevitable mass of detail that will greet you on arrival. Be mindful of other people's priorities but don't let them send you off course.

Having successfully eased yourself into your new role and gained the trust of your boss and the team, start to make things happen. First of all, focus on your leadership style and how it needs to change to suit the new role; then focus on the team. Are they the right people and, if so, what will make them work more effectively as a strategy team?

Finally, at the appropriate time, you need to think about your next career move, and whether you are interested in getting to the top by becoming a company director. It is not for everyone, as the commitment, time and associated stress can be offputting, but the sense of responsibility and leadership can be enormously rewarding.

You've concentrated on performance up until now. Now it's time to look at your Fast Track career in strategy.

6

THE FIRST TEN WEEKS

The first ten weeks in a new role are usually the most critical – get them wrong and you risk failure, get them right and you will enjoy and thrive in your new role. This applies to everyone, team members and managers alike. Different people are involved to different extents in strategy – for most it is an important part of their job, but not all of it. For a minority, all of their work is on strategy planning. Whichever your situation, you will need to establish yourself quickly and take control. And the great thing is – anything is achievable if you set out your goals at the beginning. Just because you had no involvement in strategy in your previous role doesn't mean you can't step into it in your new one. It just needs knowledge of the principles, confidence and a plan of action.

So, what do you need to do, where should you focus and what must you avoid at all costs? The Fast Track manager will seek to understand key facts, build relationships and develop simple mechanisms for monitoring and control – establishing simple but effective team processes, some to do with strategy, others to do with lines of communication. You can simplify this task by using some of the technologies discussed, but most of your work will be working with people.

Changing roles

Why is this a critical time?

Whenever you start a new role or job, whether within your existing business or joining a new company, you have an opportunity to make a positive impression on others. This will help you get buy-in for creating new plans and making changes. However, recognise that you will only get one chance to make a first impression – get the first few months wrong and it could impact your relationships with others for a very long time, creating doubters and resisters to change.

During a period of transition, the team you will be joining will normally have an open mind and be willing to try new ideas, giving you the benefit of the doubt. We often see this phenomenon when consultants are called in to resolve a critical business issue. They may say exactly the same things as the internal managers, but as outsiders their views are respected and acted upon.

This is also a period of high emotional energy and activities will often gain a higher level of enthusiasm and commitment. After all, your team is trying to make a good first impression on you too. Use this time wisely and you will gain significant advantage.

What are the potential pitfalls?

Whilst this period of transition presents opportunities to make a good impression, you will also face a number of challenges.

→ Your recent appointment to the role probably means you know less than anyone else about what the current strategy is – and what the new one should look like.

→ Your lack of knowledge and expertise makes you vulnerable to getting decisions wrong.

→ In every team there is a mixture of people and politics – you will need to get the right people on your side to drive the strategy through to implementation.

→ There will be a lot to do in a short period of time and you may get overwhelmed by it all.

→ Most effective executives rely heavily on their informal networks, but in the early stages of a new job you will not yet have built yours up.

What is the worst-case scenario?

People often give the benefit of the doubt to those who are starting a new job or joining a new team and things often go well for a period of time. If you make mistakes they will tend to forgive you. This is referred to as the 'honeymoon period'. After a period of time (the first ten weeks), you will need to start delivering results and meeting, if not exceeding, the expectations of key stakeholders. Planning, strategic or otherwise, is a most vital skill at this time. At the end of the first ten weeks, you should already have started moving into the implementation phase.

QUICK TIP *SPEND TIME AT THE SHARP END*
Spend a day every quarter with each of your main customer-facing areas – e.g. in the shop (retail), call centre or in the field (construction, installation) – to understand the real problems facing staff and customers.

The figure below identifies the need to demonstrate tangible results early on or risk failure shortly after your honeymoon period has ended. During this initial period, it is vital that you take the steps necessary to set yourself up for longer-term success, or else you run the risk of falling into the chasm.[1] This is where you make a good start but then people begin to

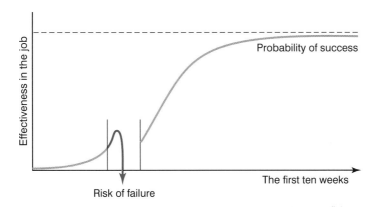

[1]Moore, Geoffrey, A. (1999 revised edition), *Crossing the Chasm*, New York: HarperBusiness.

see what you are doing as just another management initiative. Plan your first ten weeks carefully in order to set yourself up for longer-term success.

The first ten weeks

What should I do before I start?

Step one, before you do anything else, is to agree your brief. It may be from your manager, the chief executive or a governing board. Whoever it is, look for clarity on what is required and by when. From this you will be

QUICK TIP ASK YOUR BOSS
Ask your boss what they think the biggest influences will be on the company in the next year or two.

able to do your research in terms of what work is involved and what some of the potential problems are likely to be. Develop a personal to-do list of things to get ready or put in place.

Think also about how you yourself will need to change. How will you behave differently, what knowledge will you need to gain and what new skills would be useful? Understanding these things will help to build your confidence. If possible, identify key influencers in the field of strategy, such as industry experts or your internal director of strategic planning, and start to build your reputation.

What do the first ten weeks look like?

Use the following suggestions to put together a plan for your first ten weeks in your new position, whatever your role in the strategy planning process.

Week 1: Get organised

Whilst it is often tempting to rush into action, it usually pays to survey the situation carefully first. This week is about setting things up for the weeks ahead. You will only have a limited number of opportunities to impress. Rushing in without enough preparation is dangerous. The maxim 'do it once and do it right' applies.

Having said that, if this is your first week in the company, or even your first week on a new assignment, you will need to put your plan together quickly. It can be a personal plan – in other words, a plan of the key activities and results that you want to achieve personally – or it can be the business plan that relates to your new responsibilities – or both. Either way, one of your first priorities will be to identify who will help you and arrange to meet with them. Your first port of call will be to your new boss. In addition, if your predecessor is still working in the same organisation, you may consider meeting with them. You are likely to learn a lot – although that is not to say that what has gone on before should necessarily continue. You will need to make your own judgement.

Many of the managers that you need to meet will be booked up for the next couple of weeks, so try to get a place in their diary as a matter of priority. Be prepared to work long hours and travel in order to get time with these people. Look for opportunities to spend time with them outside the immediate work environment, if it makes sense. This can often produce very interesting and useful information. This is also the week to get hold of background information – to look at business reports and previous strategy documents if they exist.

QUICK TIP *KNOW YOUR BUSINESS*
Be clear on what your business performance is in terms of turnover, profit and staffing. Understand how these figures are broken down to the next level so you can discuss them confidently with other managers.

Your final priority this week, particularly if you are new to the company, is to get the housekeeping issues sorted out. You need a desk, ideally near the senior management team you will be working with. Sort out your technology, including a (laptop) computer and a good-quality phone. Attend any induction programmes that the company has in place this week if possible, or, if not, put yourself down on the list of attendees for the earliest free date. The sooner you learn about the company and its culture, the better. It will mean that you are then free to focus on the task in hand in the weeks ahead.

CASE STORY TELECOMMUNICATIONS, JOHN'S STORY

Narrator John was head of network technology for a joint venture in Indonesia. John identified early on the importance of a common set of business objectives and led the subsequent work to develop an integrated strategic plan.

Context John's company was set up with joint international and Indonesian shareholders to work with one of the key regional telecommunications operators in Indonesia. Its mission was to update the phone network and roll out telephone services to a wider market. The investment company would build the network which the national telephone company would operate.

Issue John had been recruited as head of the network roll-out. Early into his first ten weeks in the job, a conflict started to develop with the local partner over the issue of investment. The international investor wanted to implement a range of advanced technology solutions already in operation in the US and Europe. The Indonesian directors felt that the advanced technology was not the right solution for the Indonesian market. The strategy disagreement was starting to have an impact on the operational performance.

Solution John recognised early into his new role that the two teams needed to get together to address the issues. He set up an off-site meeting with the teams and an independent facilitator. The facilitator helped the two teams to understand each other's viewpoints on the business problem in hand and their respective cultural outlooks. It took several attempts for the two organisations to agree a set of common objectives, but once in place they made good progress.

Learning When two different organisations come together, it is vital that there is an atmosphere of cooperation and trust. The two teams must then agree a common set of objectives. In this case, the concerted efforts of both teams to work together eventually paid off. Behaviour changed substantially over the period of the first year as the two sides started listening more carefully to each other and moved towards a joint culture.

Weeks 2 and 3: Meet with your stakeholders

Your preparation of last week should stand you in good stead for weeks 2 and 3. Set up a few appointments for this week to meet with the key players. Prepare thoroughly and be very clear on the information you wish to find out. Draft an agenda but keep in mind the need to be flexible. This will help you get the best information from the meeting. Always take along a colleague – successful teams hunt in pairs. There are several reasons for this. First of all, you will want to listen carefully to any answers you receive and it is very difficult to write things down while picking up on the nuances of what you hear. Secondly, particularly if you are new to the organisation, your colleague will be able to pick up on some of the issues in response to your questions. Finally, if you are unable to build the rapport you expected, your colleague can take over the conversation and give you a chance to gather your thoughts and change your approach.

QUICK TIP **HAVE YOUR OWN OPINION**
Put together a list of the top five or so trends that affect your industry. Write down your opinion on each of them. If you are short on facts for some of them, put together three actions to develop your knowledge and firm up your viewpoint.

Outcomes of these meetings with key players should include the following:

1 **Their view of the business at the present time and how they see the business-wide challenges in the near and longer term.** Ask them what they think a new strategy can deliver.

2 **An understanding of their own role in the organisation and their targets for the year.** 'What keeps you awake at night?' is a good question to get a different perspective on their priorities.

3 **An insight into how strategy planning has been carried out in the past and their views on it.** Specifically, they should suggest how it can be improved and what you can do to help.

Use this meeting to outline how you propose to develop your strategy and get their agreement. Remember, it's very much an outline, so don't fence yourself in by being too specific. You will also need their commitment to attend the necessary meetings and make their people available. Your final task is to ask them if there is any further information they think is important and ask if they can suggest others who could assist you. It's always easier to get someone's cooperation when you are introduced to them by a senior manager.

Try to keep the door open (metaphorically) after each meeting. It is too easy when you have several meetings set up with new colleagues to lose the initial momentum. Copy up your notes from the meeting within 24 hours and ask for their agreement to what you have minuted. If they are key people, phone them regularly to keep them informed about your progress.

Be prepared for some surprises or even shocks. I know a woman who went into a company to produce a new strategic plan and was dismayed to find a massive industrial relations problem that was hidden from the general public and from her before she joined. Without a solution to some of the staff issues there was no hope of implementing a new strategy. She found herself working on a totally different problem from the one she thought she was hired to solve, but realised it needed to be fixed before she could even think of introducing her new plans for change.

Some time early on in week 2, you should be thinking about the high-level objectives. Objectives can be at a personal level or at a business level. Examples of personal objectives might include delivery of particular projects or personal business quotas. Examples of high-level objectives include revenue or growth targets, expansion to a new region, a requirement to diversify the product portfolio or an increased capability in a particular area. Objective setting is probably your highest priority and without it you will never be able to create your plan.

If you are setting your objectives at a personal level, it may be sufficient just to speak with your boss. If you are running a larger team, gather the stakeholders together early on to agree the high-level objectives. Do not invite too many to this first meeting – three or four of the key players should be sufficient. If you invite any more, you will never find a date when they are all free. If you do find a time for the key players to meet, you will be surprised how many of the other executives will ask to attend.

Week 4: Confirm high-level strategic themes
If you are acting as a contributor to strategy, you should use week 4 to start work on your own personal plans to meet your company

performance objectives. Your boss will probably also want you to start work on your main tasks that deliver value in your work, so plan your time carefully. By now, there should be general agreement on the process for developing strategy.

If you are developing the strategy for a business unit that you are responsible for, you will have a particularly busy week. Due to the nature of your work, you may well have a team working with you to achieve this. In this case, if you do nothing else this week except facilitate the first strategy/planning meeting, you will have met a significant objective. It is important that all participants know what they will need to bring to the meeting. Do not make it too onerous for them. In fact, you may ask them to bring nothing more than a blank sheet of paper.

Choose your venue carefully. Many strategy meetings are conducted off-site to ensure that executives are not drawn out of the meeting to solve operational crises. If you choose an off-site location, visit it before-hand or get someone else to do it for you – check out the facilities, break-out rooms, coffee/lunch break timings and directions to get there. If you are running the meeting at your office, check the logistics, including equipment such as projectors and flip charts. For such a high-level meeting, publish the agenda ahead of time. Examples of the key topics for discussion might include the following:

1 Confirmation of strategic time frame.

2 **Agreement of high-level business objectives and the strategy time frame in years.** Some companies in fast-changing businesses, such as mobile phone manufacturers, have a strategic time frame of one year. Other companies, such as mining companies and power stations, have a time frame up to 20 years.

3 **Discussion of the competitive advantage within your area of responsibility.** If you are working at a business level, this is where you would look to outline the current product marketing strategy and how priorities might change.

4 **Agreement on the schedule to create the plan and its deliverables.** This includes, of course, the date of the next meeting.

Copy up the minutes within 24 hours and contact each of the members to get their feedback and re-commitment to deliver on what they agreed to do. If any of the key executives are not able to attend, meet with them separately and update them on the outcome.

Weeks 5 and 6: Develop detailed strategic plans

After your first strategy/planning meeting, the team will start work in earnest on their own detailed plans. Circulate a template (with a completed example) for each of the groups to complete and meet with them individually to discuss progress.

Each of the team members will be collecting information from different sources to build their plans. If you are working with the sales and marketing department, you may want to start working with them to build up the product–market matrix. This will provide the key direction for the business that the other plans can align with.

Week 7: Complete detailed plans and look for better options

Each of the team members should aim to complete their component of the plan in week 7. Aim to schedule the second of your team meetings this week to discuss these draft versions.

Examples of the type of objectives for this meeting might be as follows:

1 Verify the high-level objectives from the first meeting and the forecast numbers supporting them.

2 Verify that the individual plans meet the high-level criteria defined from the first meeting.

3 Identify the priorities from all the plans together and estimate funding and resources.

4 Look at ways to 'do it better'.

When it comes to 'doing it better', look at techniques for improving the plan and reducing the risks. One useful technique is to choose a small team to role-play a competitor and develop a competing strategy. When Cable and Wireless, a UK telecoms operator, worked with Bouygues, a construction and media firm in France, to bid for the third mobile licence in France, it did just this. A sub-team developed an outline of the key advantages that each of the competitors would highlight in their bids. This allowed the consortium to strengthen its bid with counter strategies, ultimately allowing it to win the licence.

Actions and priorities should be summarised before concluding the meeting. It is all too common at these meetings, where different options were evaluated, for people to have different ideas of what was agreed. Summarising should help avoid such misunderstandings.

Once again, draw up the minutes from the meeting within 24 hours and meet with each of the stakeholders individually.

Week 8: Create high-level integrated plans and review risk

This week the individual team members should be finalising their own individual plans, ensuring that their key activities are aligned with the high-level objectives. The priority is then to integrate the different plans. In the case of a company-wide strategy, this might include, for example, aligning the information technology plan to support proposed process improvements or product launches. Take the opportunity to act as the point of coordination to receive the completed plans and circulate them as one. This avoids problems with version control. Next, separate out all the most important initiatives and create a high-level plan.

QUICK TIP WOULDN'T YOU LIKE TO KNOW?
Work with your team to make a list of the things you would like to know about your company and customers but think it is impossible to find out. Then find a way to do it!

The risk process that was initiated at the meeting in week 7 should now be formalised. Create a risk register of the top risks (up to a maximum of 20) – if too many risks are identified, the task becomes too cumbersome and usually ends up on the 'too difficult' pile. Many successful teams only manage their top ten risks. A new risk can only be swapped in when an existing one has been mitigated and can be demoted. Also make sure that the lowest risks are not swamped by the higher risks. If they are, the lower risk should be taken off for the time being. For example, if there is a serious industrial relations risk to a plan, the risk of running out of new warehouse space in the next two years pales by comparison and should be left off.

Week 9: Prepare for final strategy meeting

This week is for preparing for your final strategy meeting later in the week. For this, you will need to review all the individual plans and create a summary high-level plan. Circulate the agenda for the meeting ahead of time and identify the key areas of discussion, focusing on areas of alignment between the different plans.

The final strategy meeting should:

→ sign off the high-level objectives;

→ agree the key initiatives, how they align and the joint project plan;

→ update the risk register with key risks;

→ confirm the required resources and budget.

Once the meeting is over, you will need to circulate the minutes of the meeting and collect final (approved) versions of the plans.

The next step is to put together a communications plan that describes how everyone in the organisation will be updated about the new strategy. There are three main ways to do this.

→ **The first is a simple slide presentation, most suitable for updates to the board and management.** Start with the overview first and then go into more detail as requested by the audience. Senior management hate having to wait until the end of a presentation to find out the punchline.

→ **The second way of presenting information is the story-telling or motivational style.** You can use a few slides, but imagery is more important here, talking about the end goal and inspiring the audience to move towards the future. This type of presentation suits the 'town hall' meeting, but it requires real practice to pull it off successfully. Don't forget to give yourself enough time for questions.

→ **The third presentation style is the one-to-one meeting.** This is most helpful when a manager wants to talk to their direct reports and where there may be some aspects of the new strategy that are particularly concerning for the employees. Be prepared to take on board feedback from these meetings and incorporate them into the high-level strategy.

Week 10: Strategy sign-off and communication

The main communication activities of this week should include:

→ making a presentation of the high-level plan to all stakeholders;

→ if appropriate, setting up a 'town hall' meeting to present to a wider audience;

→ finalising and signing off the final strategy document, sending summary versions to the wider audience and, if required, posting a version on the intranet.

STOP – THINK – ACT

After reading this chapter you will be aware of how critical the first ten weeks in a new role can be to success and that there are a number of actions that you should take to increase your chances of success. Take time now to reflect on each of these ideas and put together a plan for your first ten weeks.

What should I do?	What do I need to achieve?
Who do I need to involve?	Who needs to be involved and why?
What resources will I require?	What information, facilities, materials, equipment or budget will be required?
What is the timing?	When will tasks be achieved?
	Week 1
	Week 2
	Week 3
	Week 4
	Week 5
	Week 6
	Week 7
	Week 8
	Week 9
	Week 10

Visit **www.Fast-Track-Me.com** to use the Fast Track online planning tool.

Insight-driven strategy – scoping the boundary conditions

Professor George Tovstiga

Few executives when asked to summarise their company's strategy in 40 words or less are in a position to do so. If they can't, more than likely neither can anyone else in their organisation. Organisations that lack clear and simple strategy statements are vulnerable in times when difficult choices need to be made. A well-understood, clearly communicated strategy aligns aspirations, purpose and action within the business. There is much to be said for a clear strategy statement. Collis and Rukstad[2] argue that it enables two important things: first, it makes strategy formulation so much easier because executives know what they are trying to achieve. Second, implementation of the strategy also becomes much simpler, if only because the strategy's essence can be readily communicated and internalised by everyone in the organisation.

Working with executives over the years, however, I have observed that many don't even know how to begin putting a good strategy statement in place. Most executives are not aware of all the elements required for a good strategy statement; many get entangled in the complexities of strategy and lose sight of the forest for the trees when attempting to develop one. Handling the complexity whilst at the same time producing an easily understood strategy statement is both an art and a science. But there is clearly the need for a process which leads to a well-grounded but simply explained way forward.

An insight-driven approach to strategy development provides an effective and powerful alternative to many of the approaches in circulation today. It recognises that current business reality is most often highly complex and continually changing, and that, for this reason, today's managers necessarily need to make decisions under conditions of incomplete information. Within this context, insight-driven strategy seeks to provide a framework that generates pieces of a puzzle that reflect the evolving competitive landscape, although this may often present itself only as an incomplete pattern. Incomplete (and continually changing) though it may be, this window on the competitive landscape provides the manager with a far superior basis for

[2]Collis, David J. and Rukstad, Michael (2008), 'Can you say what your strategy is?', *Harvard Business Review*, April, 82–90.

strategic decision making than most alternative approaches, since it is founded on real-time, actionable insight.

Insight-driven strategy begins with a clarification of the strategic boundary conditions.

Strategic boundary conditions map the periphery of the firm's strategy space. They define the scope and limitations of the firm's strategic intent, thereby mapping its space within which appropriate strategic options present themselves. They clarify what the firm will do; where and how it will compete. Conversely, the firm's strategic boundary conditions clearly delineate what it will not do and where it will *not* compete.

Strategic boundary conditions indicate strategic direction from two perspectives: current and future strategic response, as indicated in the figure below, which shows strategic response as a function of change in the competitive landscape. A diverse range of inputs can create the insights needed for short-term responses in a relatively stable competitive environment. But the long-term requires more blue-sky thinking. Here the use of experts in helping to develop foresight ensures that the best possible future views are obtained. Foresight studies are undertaken at a company, industry (particularly used in the electronics industry) and national level. There are clearly limits to what the firm has the capability to achieve, and the purpose of this mapping is to establish the space available for future operations.

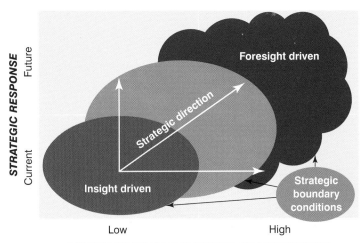

DEGREE OF CHANGE IN NATURE OF COMPETITION

Central to the derivation of the firm's strategic boundary conditions is its value proposition. The value proposition is an articulation of the firm's strategic intent and encompasses its values and aspirations, an assessment

EXPERT VOICE

of its position in its external competitive environment, and a realistic evaluation of its internal basis of competitiveness (Birchall and Tovstiga[3]). A valid value proposition guides current insight on how and where to compete most effectively today, and provides a window on appropriate strategic direction for the future based on foresight. To that end, it brings into balance the firm's strategic aspirations with its current reality. The derivation of a valid value proposition is supported by the selective application of appropriate tools of strategic analysis to generate relevant insight. Tools of strategic analysis serve solely to generate insight; they are used only very selectively and purposefully. They are not an end in themselves, as they often become in many strategy exercises that serve more to confuse than to enlighten.

Valid strategic boundary conditions therefore require a valid value proposition, one that continually challenges the industry's prevailing business logic and the firm's basic assumptions regarding its critical competing factors. Strategic boundary conditions that serve to give strategic direction with respect to competing successfully today and repositioning for future competitiveness are derived from clear, insight-driven strategic thinking.

The value and potential impact of clearly articulated strategic boundary conditions should not be underestimated. After all, they define the competitive stakes of the firm. Through clear communication, these can serve to energise and mobilise the organisation for achieving business success.

Most importantly, though, insight-driven strategic boundary conditions represent a critical first step in the development of a good strategy.

[3]Birchall, David W. and Tovstiga G. (2005), *Capabilities for Strategic Advantage – Leading Through Technological Innovation*, Basingstoke: Palgrave Macmillan.

LEADING THE TEAM

Leadership makes the difference between an effective strategy and just another paper exercise. Well-led teams are inspired to find better ways of doing things and set about achieving their aims with energy. Focus on your personal attributes as a strategic leader and reflect on what it takes to lead and develop a team.

Changing myself

Leadership roles in developing strategy

Strategic thinking has always been considered one of the key skills and differentiators of top leaders. It gives you wider visibility of your organisation and, in turn, you will be visible to a wider audience. In general, there are four leadership roles in the development of strategy.

Contributor
This is often the first role in the world of strategy. Contributors support one part of the strategy, typically as a subject matter expert or someone with a particular skill. They may provide the background information for one of the functional plans; for example, sales, finance or human resources. Contributors will often carry out the collection and analysis of information and verify that it is accurate and complete. Contributors work alongside the section leads, project managers and senior sponsors in the development of the strategy.

Section lead

The section lead is responsible for developing a particular aspect of the overall strategic plan. A typical section lead would head a small team or department. It might include procurement, human resources or information technology, or a subset of these. There would typically be a number of contributors working for the section lead to gather the background information and analysis. The section lead would then bring this together to create a consolidated plan. The section lead may also run team sessions to review the analysis and develop strategic options. They would then bring these options into the broader strategy picture.

Project lead

The project lead is responsible for the successful completion of the strategic plan. They perform many tasks within this role. First of all, they identify the project members and make sure that each can commit enough time to complete the project. Secondly, they inform each team member of the schedule and the work they need to carry out. Finally, they will keep track of the key deliverables, highlighting any risks and delays that the project might encounter and summarising them to the overall strategy lead.

Strategy lead (head of strategy development or managing director)

The strategy lead is ultimately responsible for creating the final strategic plan. Due to their size, large organisations often run a separate strategy department or function. The head of that department is responsible for collecting and integrating the lower level strategies to develop an overall corporate strategy. For most organisations, though, the head of strategy development is the managing director of the company! There is nothing more important to the future survival of an organisation than the creation of a clear and well-communicated business strategy.

The head of strategy will meet with the project lead on a regular basis, typically once a week, to discuss progress and understand any obstacles or risks on the project. They will host the meetings of the section leads, and may run workshops for the whole project. They are also responsible for ensuring that the strategy is joined up, creating, for example, a high-level plan that summarises the strategic future with clearly sequenced and prioritised milestones.

CASE STORY HOTELS AND RESTAURANTS, BEN'S STORY

Narrator Ben was part of the senior management team at Whitbread, the UK's largest hotel and restaurant business. Working with the senior management team, he developed new ways to visualise the future for hotel guests as a way of stimulating creative thinking and innovation in the company.

Context Whitbread was embarking on a new strategic planning exercise. Whitbread PLC is the UK's largest hotel and restaurant company, operating market-leading businesses in the budget hotels and restaurant sectors. Its brands include Premier Inn, Table Table (a table for any occasion), Beefeater, Brewers Fayre, Taybarns and Costa Coffee.

Issue The senior management team wanted to illustrate what might happen with technology rather than what had been planned – to try to get people to open their minds and think about new possibilities. By way of example, they looked at what the future might look like for the hotel guests. They wanted to illustrate some of the main technology innovations that were being planned and, more importantly, demonstrate how they would help the customer experience.

Solution Ben commissioned a media company to create an animation that showed a guest of the future, demonstrating how they would book their rooms and check in, and the range of new products that they could take advantage of. By animating the future world, Ben was able to paint a clear picture or 'vision' for senior managers that showed how the new developments would actually work in practice. In fact it proved valuable for all levels of the business and also with its suppliers.

Learning There is real value in helping people to visualise new changes and demonstrate how they benefit the customer. The animation not only illustrated the proposed new products and services, but also planted a clear and vivid picture in the minds of everyone who saw it.

Thinking like a leader

Whatever your role in the development of strategy, take pride in the fact that this is an extremely valuable assignment and it is a statement of the confidence and trust that your organisation has in you.

When I run strategy workshops, I ask the delegates to reflect on what they consider to be the main qualities of leaders. The discussion is slightly prejudiced by talking about politicians and sporting captains beforehand. The answers are probably what you would expect – strong character, great communication and motivation, integrity, creating a vision and so on. But when I ask them to think about the boss that they were most inspired to work for, I get different answers, such as a good listener, good sense of humour (actually the most common response), trustworthy, knowledgeable and so on. You may think this is because it is a different question, but it isn't. Leadership is about getting people to follow – in other words, inspiring them to do what is asked. This is important because it highlights the fact that the leaders of today are not necessarily figureheads. Leadership is about encouraging others to follow the right path. And in today's environment, the most important leadership behaviours are listening, being supportive, making the environment fun to work in and leading by example.

QUICK TIP CHECK IN WITH YOUR TEAM
Ask members of your team on a regular basis how relevant the strategy is for the organisation.

In practice, your leadership style will depend on whether you are in charge of the whole team, or whether you have people in the team that you are only indirectly responsible for – what is known as a virtual team. In the virtual team, you may be required to manage people, some of whom may be more senior than you. It is much more difficult to lead in these circumstances, but perversely, it is often the first leadership situation that managers have to handle. Some liken it to 'herding frogs', trying to get people to do something that is not necessarily top of their agenda, and without the ability to demand that they 'just do it!'.

The first task in a situation like this is to gain the confidence of the whole team, but particularly the senior members. They may be unaware of your background or skills and specifically why you are involved in the strategy process. Take time to get to know them, ask questions about their own work and learn from their experience. Be respectful, but don't overdo it as it might reinforce their view that you lack the knowledge or experience. On the other hand, being patronising and giving the impression of knowing everything is the fastest way of losing their commitment. Communications consultants David Gillespie and Mark Warren[1] suggest that if you were to rank your status from 0 to 10, where 0 means very humble and subservient and 10 means arrogant and overconfident, you should aim for somewhere between 5 and 7.

It is important to recognise that the environment you work in today is very different to that of, say, 20 years ago. The separated offices that all managers used to have are no longer the norm. Letters and phone calls are no longer routed through secretaries. Overall, communication in today's business environment is much more open, with anyone being able to send an email to the managing director's PC or mobile device or to phone them directly on their mobile. This has served to improve communication and, more importantly, to break down the false barriers of status. In place of hierarchies, it is much more common to see virtual teams, requiring managers to provide leadership across wider boundaries.

So being confident enough to talk to senior managers about their work and what needs to be done in the process is a good first step. Learning from the experience of others is essential, but be prepared to challenge in a positive way. And don't be easily put off. The experts on what happened in the past may not necessarily be the experts at predicting the future. You need to help them in challenging their thinking, asking if the competition do it differently and, if so, why. Careful and sensitive questioning can often reveal the real reasons why things are done the way they are and provide opportunities for improvement. Take care in the questions you ask and remember that it is not just the question but the way you ask it. This is particularly valid when using email since it is difficult to express emotions in the same way as in face-to-face communication. By way of example, asking the question 'Why did you do it this way?' sounds quite aggressive when written on paper or in an email, but less so when asked face to face.

If you are fortunate enough to be the manager of a team directly reporting to you, rather than a virtual team (for example, when developing your own functional plan), then you have a different role to play. Start by explaining the process to the team and coach them to complete their assignments. Where possible, use your network to find valuable background information and start to build support for your strategy.

---

[1] Gillespie, D. and Warren, M. (2208), *Teach Yourself the Clinton Factor: Communicating with Charisma*, New York: McGraw Hill.

QUICK TIP *IF YOU WERE IN CHARGE*
Ask some of your colleagues around the organisation what they would do differently if they were in charge.

Take a few moments to reflect on your leadership style. Do you have an authoritarian approach to leadership or a collaborative approach? Think how you might vary your style to suit different situations. As a general rule, the collaborative style is the most effective in the business environment of today. Employees expect to be involved in all the key decisions that affect them. If you use a collaborative style, expect to find higher levels of motivation in your team as they adopt and implement ideas that were at least partly their own.

There are some situations, though, where a more authoritarian approach is needed. Strategy is not about compromise and there will be many situations where you are presented with several ideas to choose from. Each idea may well stand up on its merits, but you will need to make a strategic choice. A good example might be where development of several products is being proposed by different product managers. All the proposed developments would probably yield a positive business case, but in strategy you will recognise that spreading your product development capability and consequently stretching your market capability is not a good strategic decision. You will then have to make a call on which investments are needed. Compromise agreements do not work in this case.

Thinking of the future

One of the most important changes you will need to make in your work will be your outlook. Aside from developing strategy, most managers work on day-to-day activities with deadlines a few days, sometimes weeks and occasionally months ahead. To suddenly have to work on a project that may not happen for two or three years can be a bit of a shock. In fact, the first time it happens, it requires something of a mindset change.

Many managers burn a lot of mental energy trying to think of the future. In itself, this is no bad thing, but the mistake they are making is trying to compute many different scenarios without any bounds. It is important that you create an early view of what the future might look like. Most of the time, after all the dreaming and imagining, the future is recognisable from the ways things are today, but just faster, better and cheaper. Having a simple picture of the future lets you focus your energy on clear strategies for making it happen.

Thinking of the future is essential for the three-year plan, but keep in mind what the outcome of your planning work should be. One of the most common questions I am asked at strategy workshops is, 'When will I know that I have finished?' Of course, answering the question with 'Strategy never ends' may be factually correct, but it isn't very helpful. Your team will want to know when the late nights will end and they can go back to leading a normal life. As part of your leadership role, you need to be able to answer this, describing what the completed document looks like and what sign-offs are needed.

What personal attributes will I need?

From a personal point of view, one of the most difficult things that you will need to do is to understand your strengths and weaknesses. You will need to play to your strengths and address areas of weakness, either by improving the way you do things or getting others to work on those areas. You will need to stay positive, taking time to respond where necessary, particularly if tensions are running high.

QUICK TIP CONNECTING PEOPLE

Arrange breakfast with two other managers to discuss strategy and general issues. Choose colleagues that do not necessarily know each other well and develop your reputation as someone who is 'well connected'.

In his study on what makes leaders successful, Daniel Goleman[2] noted a number of characteristics that identified leaders that were considered successful, not just in how others perceived them but also in the

[2]Goleman, Daniel (1998), *What Makes a Leader? Emotional Intelligence*, Boston, MA: Harvard Business School Press.

business results that they delivered. Interestingly, he observed that although big-picture thinking was essential when it comes to developing strategy, effective leadership called on a completely different set of skills, which he called emotional intelligence.

There are two parts to emotional intelligence – knowing and managing yourself and knowing and managing others. Your work in strategy will require you to develop all these skills. Let us start with the personal attributes you will need – knowing and understanding yourself. From the following list of personal skills, assess how well you score in each area. The best source of comparison is to look at your colleagues around you.

→ **Time management.** The ability to prioritise key activities and achieve high-quality deliverables within the timescales agreed.

→ **Analysis, problem solving and decision making.** The ability to gather necessary information for putting together a strategy, with the ability to analyse it and draw clear and fair conclusions. Strategy is rarely about compromise, and if two opposing views exist, you need to have a good decision-making process in order to make the clear and necessary decisions.

→ **Big-picture thinking.** The ability to summarise the key information and create a high-level picture, based on clear and accurate information. Summarising in this context means describing a number of more detailed concepts within sharply phrased statements that reflect the priorities of the strategic plan. Creating this summarised view is a rare skill. I often see people summarising complex concepts by showing single slide presentations with a mass of small print, as if summarising a large set of data can be done by using a smaller typeface. Instead, key concepts should be explained in simple clear pictures with short descriptions.

→ **Communication skills.** The ability to put across key concepts to a wider audience, explaining in a structured and logical way how your strategic thinking is developing. One of the most important communication challenges will be explaining the organisation's strategic vision. This will require a wide range of communication skills, from presenting to a large audience down to one-on-one discussions.

→ **Determination.** The ability to assess realistically what the problems are and find solutions to solve them. One thing that makes leaders stand out is the fact that they are always looking to do things better. They have great drive and determination and do not let obstacles get in their way, but instead single-mindedly set out to find solutions. At the same time, they recognise the real scale of difficulties and do not take on unachievable challenges.

→ **Innovative thinking.** The ability to look at problems from different angles and come up with insights and ideas for doing things differently. Part of the skill of innovation is to bring groups together with different knowledge, skills and outlooks and encourage them to think about problems differently to create new solutions.

→ **Knowledge of the company.** You will also need to be knowledgeable about the business. You will need to know what the current performance is – sales levels, profit levels and so on. Good strategic thinkers and leaders will understand both their own organisation and the competitive environment. They will instinctively know and understand the market in which they operate and the new products that will need to be developed to meet changing needs.

 QUICK TIP ARE YOU WORKING STRATEGICALLY?
Review all your activities and relate them to the strategic objectives. Identify how much of your time is spent working on strategic and relevant activities versus tactical activities.

How do I work effectively with other team members?

The most important skills for working with others are as follows.

→ **Ability to work in a team environment.** The ability to work with others in a collaborative way, sharing information and developing joint deliverables. You will need to be a diplomat but be prepared to use influence where necessary. You will need to understand what is driving the team and the strengths and weaknesses of all the players. Strategy is more akin to rugby than, say, cycling, since each member of the team will have very different characteristics, skills and roles to play.

→ **Ability to work in meetings.** Being able to structure them with clear agendas and facilitating free-talking but focused discussions on the key topics.

→ **Listening skills.** Understanding the expertise and motivation of others and encouraging them to use their skills effectively in the development of the strategy.

→ **Awareness of corporate politics.** An understanding of corporate politics in a positive sense, in that you understand who the key decision makers are and how these decisions are made. Those who understand corporate politics know that it is about having influence with these people, and that means understanding their motives. Office politics is rarely the sinister back-stabbing that many people imagine, but a good leader will be mindful that this can sometimes be the case and will seek to address it with positive leadership. Those who have good awareness of corporate politics find common ground with others and build wide networks both inside and outside the organisation.

Getting the team to work effectively

How do I get the most out of each member of my strategy team?

As a section lead or the overall head of the strategy development process, you will have team members reporting to you and looking for guidance. The following ideas will help you to lead your team effectively.

→ **Team building.** When you build your team, choose people who work well together, have good subject knowledge and yet think in different ways. Being able to build a sense of urgency within the team and generate the momentum necessary will signifi-cantly improve the way that the business is run. Look out for troublemakers and take steps to keep them out of your team.

→ **Spend time with your team.** Try to spend time with your team on a regular basis and ensure that they have the information they need to develop their part of the plan. Listen to their issues and ask questions about the data they have collected. Update them on project issues, including any high-level changes in direction and requirements for outputs. Encourage them to look at things from a different perspective, looking for better ways to solve problems and challenging the basis of how things are done today.

→ **Act as a coach.** If you are an experienced manager, develop-ing the organisation's strategy may provide you with the opportunity to coach other managers working on the project. Where possible, encourage participants to get to the right result by themselves, although be prepared to give close guid-ance for less experienced managers.

→ **Create harmony.** If you are the overall head of the project, you will most likely find that many of the team members have not worked together before. Part of your role will be to help every-one to get to know each other. Encourage everyone to meet outside the work environment from time to time so that they have informal time together.

→ **Be decisive.** Time is of the essence and you will need to get the team working together quickly – don't wait for everyone to agree whether it is a good idea, just go and do it. Often an off-site meeting will help, with a combination of team-building work and practical strategy skills development.

Focused strategy workshop

The best strategic plans usually come from a combination of individual and team working. Once your team has some initial ideas, it makes sense for everyone to meet up and discuss them. The following table presents some guidelines to make these meetings or 'strategy work-shops' effective.

ANTECEDENTS	BEHAVIOUR	CONSEQUENCES
→ Ensure it is focused on a current business imperative. → Put together an invitation to attend that includes a set of objectives and an agenda with timing (allow enough time). → Invite the right people to get the right skills and ensure they understand the processes you will be using – hold a five-minute conversation with each to clarify expectations. → Ask a member of your team to come prepared with their background thinking in order to stimulate and challenge the team. → Ensure the room you have is large enough, has plenty of natural light and room for break-outs to encourage creativity. → Send an email reminder out a few days beforehand to all invited participants. → Think about the risks – what could go wrong – and plan mitigating actions.	→ The focus is on a current business priority and generating new ideas for performance improvement. → 'Success' would be defined as a new idea that would improve performance and could be implemented within the following quarter.	→ Allow the team to present their ideas to the senior manager at the end of the session. → Allocate a budget for team-building activities as a way of encouraging future participation and celebrating success. → Arrange for someone to capture the outputs and circulate them to the team within a couple of days.

Create the right environment

Why is this important?

Creating the right environment will help you get the most out of your team. It will foster teamwork and increase productivity. As word of your successes gets round, you will find that talented people approach you and want to join your team. Success breeds success and it is important to get on the right side of the wave, taking care of all aspects that contribute to a good working environment. These include the culture and values of the organisation, the physical environment and the way the group works together as a team.

> **QUICK TIP** *BUILDING NETWORKS*
> Use your network to understand what is going on in the
> business and the priorities for the future. Ask people in
> different parts of the business how they might solve
> problems from others departments.

Which culture is best?

Different organisations create different cultures. If you are visiting a new
company, you will be able to infer a lot about the culture of the organisation by what you see around you. For example, creative design studios
might have futuristic designs on the wall, a fashion-conscious dress code
and an informal atmosphere. A traditional insurance company would tend
to be more formal, with more classical decorations and a more conven-
tional dress code. Airlines, some restaurants and other organisations have
uniforms to emphasise brand and a consistent level of quality.

Whilst the way employees dress and the look of the offices isn't the
same as culture, it is an important part of it. Culture will be represented
by everything around the organisation. Of course, there is no right or
wrong when it comes to culture, but it should be in line with what the
organisation does and what it stands for.

Values and behaviour

As part of your strategy development, the values of your organisation will
provide a strong guide for the behaviour of both you and your team. If
your values are already written down, so much the better, but you will no
doubt have an unwritten code of behaviour that people are expected to
follow. This code of values will define how people work with others, how
they do their job and even, as we saw earlier, how they dress. There is a
lot to be said for having a set of aspirational values, although be careful
not to build a set of unachievable rules that no one recognises. Most
successful blue chip organisations have maintained the same code of
values for years, sometimes decades. This code helps to define the culture of the organisation.

Culture is also defined by the behaviour of the management. By definition, therefore, you will see small changes in culture across the

organisation. As a key player in the development of strategy, you will have your own role to play here. Look to enhance communication between members of the team while at the same time encouraging them to work independently. Any successful business culture also rewards the correct behaviour. These rewards don't have to be just financial, although these are the most common and (for all the management rhetoric to the contrary) usually the most successful. Rewards can also be awards or simple recognition.

What should the physical environment look like?

It goes without saying that the quality of the work environment will affect the quality of the work produced. Yet too few organisations think carefully about what is required and what could be improved. Moving to an open-plan office has some advantages – it is cheaper for a start and it can help to bring teams together. Each team is aware of the work ethic and productivity of others and this is obviously a great driver of good performance if the overall work ethic is good. In theory, it should be much easier for team members to keep up to date with what is going on from their colleagues. The downside is that people are interrupted more often and it can be difficult to discuss private issues. Open-plan environments should be kept clutter free and care given to noise and disruption levels. People should have enough space to do their work effectively and your team members must have time to work without distractions. This can be by making meeting rooms available for private work or giving staff the option to work from home.

Often though, it is the senior management who are the ones involved in the development of strategy and it is more common that they have their own office. This has the advantage that they can discuss items of a confidential nature, but more work needs to be done to ensure collaboration on the strategy project.

Building the team

What makes a great team?

Choosing a number of great individuals to play together in a team does not necessarily make a great team – as the coaches of many international teams have discovered. The analogy of an international football team is a good one. In your strategy team, the organisation will have chosen its best minds to identify the right future and help build it. But even though each of the team members has been successful in their own functional disciplines, this is no guarantee that the team will bond and work successfully together. Team members need time to get to know each others' styles and you will need a range of those styles to be successful.

The strategy team is an elite team, comprising the best thinkers and most influential people from your organisation. Building team strength with such a diverse set of skills takes time. Team building has four stages:

FORMING	STORMING	NORMING	PERFORMING
The teams gets together for the first time	Team members get to know each other	The team shares ideas and builds a better way forward	Team members put the ideas into practice and deliver results

→ Forming – where the team gets together for the first time.

→ Storming – referring to brainstorming, where team members are confident about creating and sharing new ideas together, building on the individual skills of the team members to come up with a better solution; this is sometimes called the 'middle way' or 'creating a win-win'.

→ Norming – where team members start to adopt the common way of working and agree their priorities, following the storming phase.

→ Performing – where team members start to work within the common idea of the team and take the new ideas outside the team to put them into practice.

QUICK TIP **WHAT IS HAPPENING WITH TECHNOLOGY?**
Take time once a quarter to review the latest technologies and look for ways to use them to improve the effectiveness of your team.

Fast Track strategy teams can be identified by the following five skills.

1 **The team will have great clarity in its goals and a real sense of purpose.** Fast Track strategy teams will often be remembered long after the work is complete as providing a foundation for the continued success of the organisation.

2 **The team will have a strong and enthusiastic leader who provides direction, is supportive of team members and willing to shoulder responsibility when things do not go according to plan.** All team members will bring their own expertise and will be providing leadership in whatever role they play.

3 **Fast Track teams accept that things will change and are flexible.** They will actively look out for obstacles that lie on the road to success and develop solutions together to overcome them.

4 **They will have a feeling of shared responsibility and be supportive of each other.** They will take time out to learn and develop new skills – both individually and as a team. They keep a close eye on how they are performing and observe other similar teams in order to identify alternative approaches that could be adopted.

5 **The team will be balanced in terms of the skills and capabilities of its members and in terms of the roles they each fulfil.** There will be people capable of creative challenge, but also people willing to get their heads down in order to put the work in and deliver the results.

How do I overcome barriers to change?

Strategy is all about setting a new direction and often means embarking on a journey of significant change. There is an emotional aspect to changing the way that things are done that is well recognised. The figure opposite illustrates the sort of emotions that are common in most change projects. It divides the change project into four main phases.

1 **Phase one.** The business carries on as usual, often thinking that things are progressing quite well. It can take a strong jolt to embark on a path for change.

2 **Phase two.** A sense of urgency has been created, leading to the formation of the Fast Track strategy team. This acts as the catalyst to discuss new and radical ways to change the way things are currently done. The wider organisation may struggle to come to terms with this and can be obstructive in the development of new ideas.

3 **Phase three.** The team continues to encounter problems, but looks for positive ways to solve them. Time is spent communicating with the rest of the organisation and canvassing for new ideas.

4 **Phase four.** Proposed changes gain credence and support as people realise the seriousness of previous problems and the benefits that the new proposals will have in providing a future of sustained success.

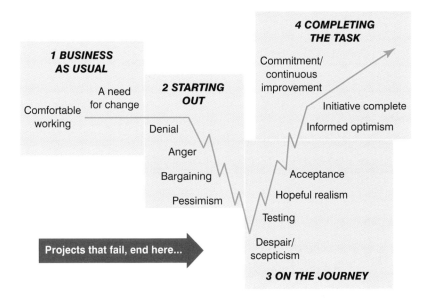

These four stages reflect the problems that you may encounter in developing the strategy itself. But once your strategy is developed, understood and embraced, the real work will start. You will experience the same cycle of change, only on a bigger scale, as the organisation tries to implement it.

QUICK TIP COMMUNICATING STRATEGY

Don't fall into the trap of thinking that people want to hear all the background of how you reached your decisions. Let them know the result quickly and then listen to see whether they have any questions.

STOP – THINK – ACT

This chapter has presented ideas for managing and developing your team. This will be key to your success as you will not be able to achieve your objectives working alone. Successful strategy planning and implementation is often achieved via cross-functional teams where you will not necessarily have direct control.

Stop and reflect on how well you are leading your strategy team and look for ways you could improve. Think about how well the team is performing and where the team is in the 'forming to performing' model.

What should we do?	What actions do we need to take to build the team?
Who do we need to involve?	Who needs to be involved and why?
What resources will we require?	What level of investment would be required?
What is the timing?	What deadlines do we need to meet?

Visit www.Fast-Track-Me.com to use the Fast Track online planning tool.

Making it happen – the facilitation bit

Dr Jean-Anne Stewart

EXPERT VOICE

"Why do so many business strategies and initiatives fail to get off the ground? Companies spend millions on consultants that come up with strategies to increase innovation, productivity and profitability, but so often these just end up in reports gathering dust on the shelves. Sometimes it is not external consultants but groups of bright and motivated employees that have great ideas which could be usefully integrated into strategy, but still too often nothing happens.

This is where facilitation comes in. But before going any further, it is necessary to clarify what is meant by this overused and frequently misunderstood term. Facilitation simply means 'to make easy' or 'to enable'. In organisational terms, this typically means a person called a 'group facilitator' who works with a group or team to help them achieve their objectives. The facilitator does not get involved in the content of the group discussions and decisions, but works with them to design and manage the group process in a balanced and impartial way.

So when do you use facilitation? The facilitation process is most applicable to meetings or workshops where the group needs to come up with new ideas, strategies and plans. If a manager needs to communicate pre-decided initiatives and plans, they should make presentations or send memos. In today's organisations, people are grappling with complex business problems, new technology and complicated business processes, where it is unlikely that one leader or manager has all the answers. A facilitated group workshop can bring together people with a variety of expertise so that they can discuss strategic issues and work together in the light of their experiences. This will always come up with a higher-quality and more operationally feasible solution. There is also much greater ownership of the agreed decisions and solutions, because the group members have all been involved in putting it together and are fully aware of the thinking behind the plan or solution.

There is currently much discussion about organisational leaders being facilitators. The issues raised by this question can be illustrated by an example of a major British airline, which recognised the power of facilitation to help improve project design, planning and delivery. Initially they employed external consultants to act as group facilitators for their team meetings, group workshops and strategic planning days. They then went on to train selected employees in facilitation skills. This worked well in two ways. According to one senior manager:

Since my facilitation training, I have used more and more facilitation techniques in my normal team meetings. I find that I can manage the discussion more effectively and I pay attention to the meeting process so that we can meet our objectives. One of my team mentioned that my meetings are much more productive nowadays – they are also noticeably so!

Another said:

As a manager of a busy operational area, I recognise the need for facilitation to make sure that our meetings make good use of the team's valuable time. We cannot afford to take people off the line to waste time in poorly managed meetings. However there are some workshops that are really important and I want to take a full part in the discussion. In this situation, I will ask a trained facilitator from another part of the business to take the role of facilitator.

So whilst there are obvious benefits to using facilitation for specific workshops and meetings, not everybody has the natural ability to facilitate. There are essential interpersonal and process skills that need to be developed to be effective, whether as a facilitator or as a leader using a facilitative approach in their organisation. Facilitation of high-level strategy meetings can be particularly problematic as those involved often have conflicting personal agendas that do not always surface but which interfere with progress towards consensus.

8

GETTING TO THE TOP

Those who are involved in developing strategy are invariably those on a career fast track. Managers start their involvement in strategic development as a contributor, moving on to be a functional head before being asked to run the whole process and eventually becoming the person ultimately responsible for the strategy and its outcomes – the managing director.

To understand where you are in your 'strategic development curve', think carefully about the work you are doing in the context of strategy. Identify what it is that will make a difference in these areas – those skills and activities that will enable you to stand out. An important behaviour is 'being visible' or developing presence across your organisation. Ask yourself questions about how many of the managers you know in the company and how well they know you. Someone who is highly developed in this area would be on good terms with all the managers, a good number of them outside work. Someone who is less developed would probably know one or two managers from each department and very few socially.

I am constantly surprised as to how few managers do this self-assessment, not just of their network, but also of the other important strategy skills, such as innovative thinking, leading change and so on. If you look around your organisation, you will see many highly capable managers who are doing a job way below their abilities and potential. In particular, you may see others who strike you as better suited to the strategic role you have been given. It is certainly worth asking yourself how this happens and what needs to be done to avoid finding yourself in this situation at some later date. The point is that few managers think carefully about what they do, the impact of their actions in the organisation and how others perceive those actions.

> **QUICK TIP MANAGE YOUR KNOWLEDGE**
> Create your own strategy knowledge base. Every time you read an article or book on strategy, summarise the key points against the appropriate stage of strategy development.

So you now have a unique opportunity to do this. Rate your current performance against each of the key skills listed on pages 144–6. Choose another manager, either at your peer level or one or two levels more senior. Rate them against each of the skills. It is important that you give supporting reasons for any rating you give yourself and your comparison group.

You may well be surprised at how little difference there is between yourself and them. In fact, studies show that many of the differences are around the area of personal networks both inside and outside the organisation. If you reflect back on the attributes of emotional intelligence, this is not particularly surprising. By carrying out the assessment above, you are already on the path to understanding your own strengths and weaknesses and taking actions to play to your strengths and address weaknesses. Now you can focus on team building and networking. Working on these key areas means you are on the track to thinking and acting like a director.

Focus on performance

Fast Track managers know what is important and what is not. They focus on the key performance indicators (KPIs) that have the greatest impact on what they are trying to achieve. At all times, they understand where they are, what the bottlenecks are and how to clear them. They regularly take time to reflect on the past in order to learn from what went well or what could be improved. Likewise they think ahead to the future so that concerns can be resolved before they become crises. By always delivering against expectations, they stand out from the pack and will be automatically considered for promotion at the appropriate time.

Performance snapshot: past–historic

There is a universal complaint from historians that politicians don't learn from the lessons of history. This tends to be true of businesses as well. Without a clear understanding of what has happened before, we risk repeating mistakes from the past, or reacting to a crisis that doesn't actually exist – 'fixing what's not broken'.

 CASE STORY MAINTENANCE SERVICES, CATHERINE'S STORY

Narrator Catherine was head of operations for a maintenance services company, based in Australia. As part of a new strategy alignment, she was asked to look at the unit cost of all individual transactions as a way of identifying opportunities for improvement.

Context A maintenance client in Australia with a good reputation for quality was looking for ways to increase process efficiency as part of an overall strategic review. Catherine's team was asked to identify all the key processes within the organisation, how often that process was carried out each day and the unit cost of each transaction.

Issue The previous time this assessment had been carried out, the engineer utilisation and efficiency looked quite good. However, when the review was done a second time, the sum of the individual costs did not add up to the total costs. It transpired that the first review had not included the full cost of external contractors or the administration costs of the engineering visits. When the company benchmarked itself against similar organisations, it found that the engineer costs were 25 per cent higher than the industry average.

Solution Following Catherine's advice engineers were trained to do both the installation and maintenance work. Rotas could then be optimised to reduce travel time and costs. This allowed the number of external contractors to be reduced. The installation and maintenance administration was also combined, delivering additional savings.

Learning For a medium or large company, it is important to understand the cost base, in particular which processes are efficient and which are expensive. It is important to have independent assessment and benchmarking to put it into context. Through proper identification of costs, the company could develop strategies to maintain the quality of service but reduce the associated costs.

So, review your strategy KPIs and assess how well you performed in the last period, what the trend was and perhaps what the specific problems were. This goes into the information pot for the next version of the plan.

Many organisations maintain a 'lessons-learned' database but then rarely use it. The trouble is that they are easy to set up but not always easily accessible to those who need them. Think how you would find out about what has happened in your organisation in the past.

By way of example, at a recent project management training session for a large manufacturing company, the participants were asked how they learned from previous mistakes. They stated that it took them two days to identify databases that might contain useful information and another two days to get security clearance to look at the data, and even then the data was unstructured and therefore of little value. Once the manager had left the room, they all admitted that they just didn't bother any more and started with a blank piece of paper.

QUICK TIP *WHO HAS THE INFLUENCE?*
Put together a list of the top ten most influential people in your company. Look at how they have built their influence and see how you can emulate their success. Look for opportunities to talk to them and find out more about how they have achieved it (top managers spend up to 50 per cent of their time networking).

Performance snapshot: present – current situation (gap)

The organisation's strategy champions have to focus on the right priorities. If they don't, then they risk turning a problem into a crisis. They will want to know:

→ what is currently going on – what strategy projects are under way;

→ whether they are on track;

→ if not, what are the issues and who is dealing with them?

They want this information in a specific way, not as a series of vague intentions. They might use the SMART acronym by saying they want information on projects that is specific, measurable, accurate, relevant and timely.

Performance snapshot: future – predictive

Of course, you can't measure your future performance directly. But the essence of strategy is to help you work on activities today that will make you successful in the future. With your strategy in place, ensure that it stays aligned to the business priorities, taking into account the changing environment. Keep a look out for predictions of the future that might stand in the way of success.

One of the best ways to do this is through risk analysis. Look carefully through your risk register and think about what needs to be done. What other threats are appearing on the horizon that need to be included? Maintain an awareness of which projects are likely to succeed and which are likely to fail so that you can be ready to deal with the casualties – both the projects and the people working on them!

QUICK TIP CREATIVE TIME
Look for ways of stopping activities that don't add value in order to free up time for creative thinking.

In summary, think ahead, plan ahead and stay ahead.

Invite challenge

Who can we get to challenge us?

Fast Track managers never rest on their laurels. You may think that your performance is on track, but as the external business environment changes you need to adapt. Look for ways to introduce challenge for yourself and your team on a regular basis, aiming to bring in ideas, tools and techniques from recognised strategy leaders. Review the following different groups.

→ **Other internal teams.** What ideas can be shared? What common risks can be avoided?

→ **Customers.** How are their requirements changing? What future scenarios might occur?

→ **Competitors.** What are they doing now that could be emulated?

→ **Supply chain.** What possibilities are there for improved effectiveness and efficiency?

→ **Partners.** What can we learn from them? What opportunities are there for collaboration?

→ **Industry advisers.** What are the experts recommending? What breakthrough tools and techniques have they developed?

Engage in challenging acts on a regular basis, even if you don't need to in order to meet your KPIs because you're ahead of the game. If you are finding it easy to meet the targets set for you then don't wait for your boss to extend them – do it yourself. Perhaps take time to get involved in areas where you are not confident in order to continuously develop yourself.

Remember to use relevant opportunities for self-development both inside and outside work, within your function and without. Consider the following areas:

→ Get involved in public speaking, such as presenting at conferences and seminars.

→ Commission external studies – for example, by using under-graduate students.

→ Get involved in an outside body involved with key industry issues.

→ Get on to the steering committee for a professional institute.

→ Respond to public enquires (from the government) and try to get on review bodies by developing a reputation.

→ Get on internal working parties investigating company issues but possibly outside the strategy project area.

How do I keep up to date?

As well as working with other groups inside and outside the business, think carefully about what additional sources of knowledge and insight you want to receive and how often. There is a wealth of information available from a variety of sources, so you need to be selective, as the time you have available for reading is limited and the quality can be variable.

QUICK TIP *KEEP UP TO DATE*
Review the financial pages on a regular basis (e.g. *Financial Times*) and subscribe to one of the top strategy journals (e.g. *Harvard Business Review*).

→ **Web.** This provides freely available information from a variety of sources but is typically unstructured and will contain bias. *Fast Track recommendation: review the websites of your 'top ten' customers and competitors twice a year and identify up to five other useful websites that provide challenge.*

→ **Journals or trade magazines.** These are available via a subscription and will make the latest ideas and thinking available but will often contain a lot of commercial advertorials. *Fast Track recommendation: subscribe to the one journal of greatest relevance to your industry for one year and review its value. Once you have read it, circulate it to other members of your team.*

→ **Conferences.** These provide a useful opportunity to listen to stimulating presentations and are typically an excellent way of networking with others outside the business, but they can be time consuming and expensive. *Fast Track recommendation: identify the one conference of greatest relevance to your industry and attend it for two consecutive years. Aim to identify at least three people (other attendees or presenters) to follow up with about specific issues you have.*

→ **Communities of practice.** These are online discussion forums between like-minded people within the industry community. *Fast Track recommendation: these can be extremely useful or a* *complete waste of time, so give them a go and see what value you get. You may also want to consider forming your own forum, but recognise that you will need to put in the necessary time and effort to get it off the ground.*

→ **Benchmarking.** This is perhaps the most valuable way of identifying new ideas and stretching the way you think, but the process takes effort to set up and manage. *Fast Track recommendation: definitely worth doing, so identify two or three other organisations that you respect as being strategy innovators and meet with them up to four times a year. Make sure you use a facilitator and follow a structured agenda to maximise the cross-company learning. Remember that you will have to give value to them as well as the other way round.*

→ **Professional bodies.** Membership of these bodies becomes more important the more senior you become and these bodies are often a source of free advice. *Fast Track recommendation: once you have been in your role for at least a year, sign up for an initial trial period and see what benefits you receive.*

→ **Fast-Track-Me.com.** All the key ideas, tools and techniques contained in the Fast Track series are available via the internet at **Fast-Track-Me.com**. *Fast Track recommendation: firstly, allocate 30 minutes to visit and explore the site. It contains a rich source of tips, tools and techniques, stories, expert voices and online audits from the Fast Track series.*

Remember that whatever your source of information, to maximise the benefits you need to put time aside and make the necessary effort. However, also recognise that you will never have perfect knowledge – particularly in the area of strategy. Decide what level of certainty will be good enough and then act on it.

Getting promoted

At the appropriate time the Fast Track manager will seek promotion again. This may occur within a few months or possibly a number of years, but in either case take time to reflect on your state of readiness.

Identify the future role you are keen to fulfil, clarify the criteria you will need to satisfy in terms of skills, experience, attitudes and behaviours, and consider how you will visibly demonstrate these attributes to others. Ask yourself the following questions.

→ **Capability.** Do I have what it takes in terms of what I have achieved and learned so far?

→ **Credibility.** Can I convince others that I can and will perform the role well?

→ **Desire.** Do I want the role and do I have sufficient drive and enthusiasm to do a great job?

→ **Relationships.** Do I have positive working relationships with the right people?

→ **Competitiveness.** Am I the most appropriate candidate, given the internal and external alternatives?

If you have concerns, then put in place a plan to address them. Timing will be key so prepare well before putting yourself forward for the role.

QUICK TIP *TOP NETWORKERS*
Look around your organisation and identify those who have strong networks. Look to see how they operate and think how you can use your existing network to build new alliances.

Becoming a director

What is the role of a director?

Few organisations have the formal title of strategy director, but most will have a member of the executive team nominated to develop the strategic plan – sometimes it is the CEO, who of course retains the ultimate responsibility for strategy, but often the plan is run by someone in the CEO's office. In some organisations this will be the marketing director, in others it will be the R&D director or director of operations. Whatever their actual title, the director of strategy will fulfil various roles in addition to meeting their statutory responsibilities, including:

→ setting the overall business strategy and gaining the active support of all members of the board;

→ developing clear and achievable strategy, ensuring that sufficient budget and resources are assigned to meet objectives in the face of competition;

→ ensuring that members of the board are aware of critical market and technology trends, the impact of each on business performance and the implications in terms of driving fundamental change;

→ designing the overall strategic development framework and putting in place the appropriate review and governance processes to ensure effective implementation;

→ reporting on strategic progress and performance to the board, conducting stakeholder presentations and briefing key opinion leaders inside and outside the organisation.

What will my statutory responsibilities be?

As a member of the board of directors, you will have a number of roles and statutory duties that will require your involvement in:

→ determining the company's strategic objectives and policies;

→ monitoring progress towards achieving the long-term objectives and policies;

→ directly appointing or supporting the recruitment of all high-level managers directly involved in setting strategy;

→ accounting for the company's activities to relevant parties, e.g. shareholders;

→ attending board meetings that run the company, displaying the high level of integrity that is inferred by statutory standards and the company's interpretation of corporate governance, particularly in sensitive areas such as health and safety.

You will also have to conduct yourself in a highly professional manner.

→ A director must not put themselves in a position where the interests of the company conflict with their personal interest or their duty to a third party.

→ A director must not make a personal profit out of their position as a director unless they are permitted to do so by the company.

→ A director must act bona fide in what they consider is in the interests of the company as a whole and not for any other purpose or with any other agenda.

Planning your exit strategy

At some stage you will want to change role. You may be moving into a different function, getting your boss's job or simply retiring, but whatever the situation, the way you manage the transition is critical to sustaining the performance of your team. This is particularly important if you are considering taking members of your team with you. Take time to plan the last ten weeks in your current role to the same level of detail as you did the first ten weeks, ensuring that your successor is well prepared and excited about taking on the new role.

What is succession planning?

Succession planning is about making sure that there is someone capable and qualified to take on your role when you leave a post. As soon as you have successfully completed your first ten weeks, start to think about who will be your natural replacement. Remember that it may take at least two years to develop their skills and experience. There may be more than one internal candidate or it may be that none will meet the criteria, but in either case your succession is important and you need to plan it in advance.

Handover tips

At the point of transition, manage the handover to your successor effectively, ensuring that you transfer knowledge (both explicit and implicit) and relationships smoothly. Take time to prepare a handover document. Then focus on people and key relationships, taking time to introduce your successor face to face rather than simply sending around an email. Take time to reflect on your original vision and how well you achieved it, then capture a list of lessons learned and add it to your handover notes.

Then start all over again

One of the great things about strategic planning is that you will be able to build on the skills you learn throughout your career. I emphasise the importance of building your own knowledge in each of the ten steps of the strategy planning process. Keep a log of your lessons learned so that you will have them the next time you embark on a 'first ten weeks' project.

STOP – THINK – ACT

In this final chapter you will have identified what you need to do to get to the top in your chosen career. Your company may not have a director of strategy per se, but strategy is the top priority of the board of directors. Stop and reflect on your career aspirations – what do you want to be doing in three years' time?

My vision	What do I want to be doing in three years' time?
My supporters	Whose support will I need to get there?
My capabilities	What capabilities and experience will I need to succeed?
My progress	What milestones will I achieve along the way?

Visit **www.Fast-Track-Me.com** to use the Fast Track online planning tool.

Where does innovation fit into strategy?

Dr Rebecca Steliaros

EXPERT VOICE

As companies face up to a period of worldwide recession, innovation activity is likely to be affected by the need to squeeze costs. Many new initiatives are likely to be put on hold as capital expenditure is curtailed. But this is the very time when organisations should be considering, at a strategic level, how they are going to move rapidly ahead as the economy improves. Key questions for the strategists are, where will the next breakthroughs come from and how can the firm be part of them? In building strategy, an understanding of the changing innovation process, particularly a move to 'open innovation' (i.e. looking outside the organisation for innovation), is important if innovation is to play a role in the strategy.

As in other areas of business activity, open networking and partnering have been shown to have a positive impact. In particular, they have been associated with better and higher levels of innovation, leading to advances in the ecosystem (including technology standards) which build the entire market and 'more and more chief technology officers at major corporations recognise they need to be part of a community that is exchanging intellectual property (IP) rather than having closed walls around their R&D labs'.[1] Open innovation has gained popularity recently as a way to achieve the short-term financial results demanded by highly competitive markets with the radical innovation provided by long-term innovation, allowing teams of companies to achieve proportionally more, especially during recession. Open innovation is about in-sourcing creativity rather than outsourcing R&D. Economic pay-off is greater for firms facing intense competition, and although the trend began in large corporations like Procter & Gamble, General Motors and IBM, medium-sized firms are also now adopting the concept. Links with external knowledge have also been shown to have a positive effect on small firms.

Long-term innovation, associated with difficulty to copy and therefore longer-term, sustainable competitive advantage, was traditionally supported via large corporate R&D functions that conducted most of the research within an industry and accrued most of the profits. Competition required massive investment in internal R&D capability and capacity. However, through open innovation that is no longer the case; new firms such as

[1]Blau, J. (2006), 'Open innovation goes global', *Research Technology Management*, Sep–Oct, 4–5.

Cisco, who tend to buy in or partner to procure technology as needed, have shown that research leaders (such as Lucent, who inherited Bell Laboratories) can be beaten without huge R&D budgets. Open innovation also offers a route for companies to avoid false negatives (i.e. avoid a lack of investment in projects which do not deliver to the core strategy of the organisation and yet could form very large markets of their own). For example, Chesbrough[2] describes how Xerox invented ethernet and the graphical user interface (GUI) and yet made no profit from it as others developed the ideas and profited accordingly. Instead, open innovation promotes proactive management of IP (intellectual property) as a way to achieve higher returns on the billions spent on R&D in big, high-tech firms every year.

Open innovation is only sustainable where its value creation is coupled with value capture.[3] In some parts of the software industry this has been achieved by the development of new business models, including selling hardware incorporating open-source software, add-ons and extensions, dual licences, consulting, etc.

To implement open innovation successfully you need to do the following.

→ **Transfer ideas within the business.** How will you ensure that shorter-term focused business units use them?

→ **Analyse and understand the whole innovation ecosystem –** don't 'offer a Ferrari in a world without gasoline or highways'.[4] Who else needs to develop what, for your innovation to succeed?

→ **Manage your own IP security.** How will you manage it? Perhaps not all IP has the same protection; or IP is viewed as a source of revenue; or IP libraries are centralised and secured.

→ **When building partnerships, manage the IP.** If appropriate avoid lawyers at the initial stages, perhaps starting with a letter of intent, until it is clear what the inputs and outputs will be.

→ **Find the right partner/(s).** This can be extremely time consuming: are there intermediaries or government research support agencies? Often it is the case that those with the problem don't know where to look for the solution so they use up money and time discovering something that's already readily available.

[2]Chesbrough, H.W. (2003), *Open Innovation: The New Imperative for Creating and Profiting from Technology*, Boston, MA: Harvard Business School Press.
[3]Chesbrough, H.W. and Appleyard, M.M. (2007), 'Open innovation and strategy', *California Management Review*, 50 (1), 57–76.
[4]Adner, R. (2206), 'Match your innovation system strategy to your innovation ecosystem', *Harvard Business Review*, April, 98–107.

→ Change the internal culture from 'not invented here' to 'proudly found elsewhere'.

→ Overcome the time gap between implementation and results. Although much shorter than increasing internal long-term research capacity, any time gaps are noticeable.

→ **Ensure your staff have the skills.** Your own people need to be extroverts who are comfortable with collaboration, have both a technical and a business mindset and are entrepreneurial.

→ Identify your primary needs and develop the ability to state problems very clearly.

→ Create a common vision.

→ Work around a big idea with clear goals.

→ Establish physical (temporary for use at the beginning of the project and at important decision-making points) and virtual meeting places.

→ Create a new mindset.

Those companies seeking to move forward through being strong innovators need to examine their strategy to see how a more open innovation model can be made to work within the enterprise.

EXPERT VOICE

PART D

DIRECTOR'S TOOLKIT

In Part B we introduced some core tools and techniques that can be used from day one in your new role as a team leader or manager with some responsibility for strategy. As you progress up the career ladder to the role of senior manager, and as your team matures in terms of their understanding and capabilities, you will want to introduce more advanced or sophisticated techniques.

Part D provides a number of more advanced techniques developed and adopted by industry leaders – helping you to differentiate from your competitors.

	TOOL DESCRIPTION
T1	Team strategy audit
T2	Strategy project checklist

T1 TEAM
STRATEGY AUDIT

Use the following checklist to assess the current state of your team. Consider each criterion in turn and use the following scoring system to identify current performance:

0 Not done or defined within the business: unaware of its importance to strategy management

1 Aware of area but little or no work done in the business

2 Recognised as an area of importance and some work done in this area

3 Area clearly defined and work done in the area in terms of strategy management

4 Consistent use of best practice tools and techniques in this area across the business

5 Area is recognised as being 'best in class' and could be a reference for best practice

Reflect on the lowest scores and identify those areas that are critical to success and flag them as status Red, requiring immediate attention. Then identify those areas that you are concerned about and flag those as status Amber, implying areas of risk that need to be monitored closely. Green indicates areas that are on track.

ID	CATEGORY	EVALUATION CRITERIA	SCORE	STATUS
STR1 Strategic planning – leadership			**0–5**	**RAG**
A	Strategy executive	A member of the executive team has responsibility for the effective and efficient introduction of strategy across the business	☐	☐
B	Stakeholders	The stakeholders involved in the development of strategy are known and they are committed to the process	☐	☐
C	Process and timetable	The strategy framework has been agreed, with a timetable for the completion of the process steps	☐	☐
STR2 Strategic focus – objectives and values				
A	High-level objectives and themes	There is a set of high-level objectives and guiding principles for setting strategy	☐	☐
B	Values and beliefs	There is a set of values which guide behaviour in the organisation and help to define the culture	☐	☐
C	Balanced objectives	There is a series of objectives looking to achieve results for the customer, improve internal processes, develop staff skills and effectiveness and deliver financial performance	☐	☐
STR3 Understanding of the business environment				
A	Competitive	There is a good understanding of the competition and how the competitive forces in the market may change over the strategic time frame	☐	☐
B	Environmental	There is a good knowledge of the political, economic, social, technological, environmental and legislative forces (PESTEL) that could have an impact on business success	☐	☐
C	Internal	There is a clear understanding of the performance of the internal organisation in all areas, ideally benchmarked against best practice	☐	☐

ID	CATEGORY	EVALUATION CRITERIA	SCORE	STATUS
STR4 Keeping ahead of the competition			0–5	RAG
A	Products and markets	The business has defined which products and services to offer to which customers and markets in the future and has clear areas of focus and boundaries	☐	☐
B	Sources of differentiation	The business has a clearly defined unique selling proposition (USP) and understands what sets it apart from its competition	☐	☐
C	Sales alignment	Sales and marketing activities as well as products and brands are aligned to the strategy	☐	☐
STR5 Matching key capabilities to strategic priorities				
A	Internal processes	A clear plan is in place to continually improve the internal processes of the business, with sufficient resources allocated	☐	☐
B	Supply chain	The strategic sourcing and supply chain processes are aligned to deliver against the strategic priorities	☐	☐
C	Skills and staffing	The organisational structure, skills and expertise of the people are correctly matched to the achievement of strategic goals, with development plans in place to address any shortfalls	☐	☐
STR6 Creating practical strategic plans				
A	Strategic plan	Clear plans have been developed from the strategic analysis to achieve the objectives. Plans are communicated across the whole organisation in a simple and understandable way	☐	☐
B	Resources and budgets	Sufficient resources and budget are allocated to strategy projects to maximise the probability of success – implementation activities are not thrown on top of the day-to-day activities	☐	☐
C	Issues and risk management	Issues and risks are proactively identified, assessed and mitigated before they become crises	☐	☐

ID	CATEGORY	EVALUATION CRITERIA	SCORE	STATUS
STR7 Commitment and ownership			0–5	RAG
A	Involvement	All levels of the organisation are involved in the development of strategy and able to contribute ideas and insights		
B	Owned at all levels	The output of the strategic planning process is owned at all levels (through strategy champions, chief strategy officer, project or programme manager). There is a 'line of sight' between the high-level strategic goals and the invidual objectives of all staff		
C	Learning culture	There is a continuous learning culture and effective knowledge management, ideally supported by internal IT systems		
STR8 Communication				
A	Strategy documentation	The strategy is fully documented and covers all the key components of the plan, including the business objectives, strategic themes, target products and markets, and strategic plans		
B	Available	The strategy is available for all employees to access and read, and is easily understandable		
C	Communicated	All stakeholder groups are made aware of the strategy and its implications, and are regularly updated of any changes		
STR9 Culture of strategic change				
A	Supportive culture	There is a culture that supports strategic thinking and a constant desire to do things better		
B	Alignment and change	The company takes on strategic change with enthusiasm, ensuring that new initiatives are aligned with strategic priorities		
C	Performance system	There is a reward and recognition system (not necessarily financially based) that encourages the adoption of strategic business change		

ID	CATEGORY	EVALUATION CRITERIA	SCORE	STATUS
STR10 Performance management			**0–5**	**RAG**
A	Agreed key performance indicators	Each strategic project has clear and agreed key performance indicators and return on strategy investment targets	☐	☐
B	Clear review process and visibility of performance	A review process for monitoring progress exists, where key stakeholders will meet to review the strategy portfolio as a whole. The senior management team has full visibility and control of the strategy process anywhere, anytime	☐	☐
C	Learning	Insights and lessons learned are captured and fed into future teams in order to maximise strategy effectiveness and avoid repeating mistakes	☐	☐

For each element of the checklist, add up the scores of the three related questions and divide by 3 – this will give you an average score for that specific element. Here is an example:

ELEMENT	SCORE	0	1	2	3	4	5	NOTES
Strategic leadership	2.1			■				No clear strategy
Strategic focus	4.2					■		
Business environment	3.6				■			Analysis not yet complete
Competitive knowledge	4.6					■		
Priority alignment	1.7		■					Activities not yet aligned with goals
Practical plans	2.6			■				No integrated plan exists
Ownership	4.6					■		
Communication	1.8		■					
Change culture	4.4					■		
Performance management	3.8				■			

In your strategy framework, the whole strategy process is only as good as each individual element. If one link in the chain is weak then the strategy process within the company will not operate to optimum efficiency and there is an increased risk of failure. The action plan, therefore, should be to focus attention and resources on the elements of greatest weakness. This approach optimises the use of resources and sets up a process of continuous improvement.

In the example above, the managers conducting the strategy audit have identified that the weakest link is that of the *priority alignment* (score 1.7). Given the sequence of events, it makes sense to complete the *business environment analysis* (score 3.6) first before going on to address the *priority alignment* and *practical plans* (score 2.6). Once the senior management team has confidence that these areas are complete, attention can be directed at improving *communication* (score 1.8).

T2 STRATEGY PROJECT CHECKLIST

What process can we follow to implement ideas?

There is no one right or wrong answer to this, and the stages and gates will vary enormously depending on the industry, the size of the business and the complexity of the project. Some new ideas can be implemented quickly and simply – for example, radically changing the pricing policy could possibly be achieved by one person over the period of an hour. However, if the strategy is to expand into Europe, then a five-minute chat over lunch is probably insufficient. Spend an appropriate amount of time planning, and where possible, use simple checklists to make sure everyone is following a common approach based on best practice.

What is a typical workplan?

The table overleaf reflects the generic tasks that would be included in each stage of a strategy project. Not all will be applicable to all projects, and many will need to be adapted to suit your business and your specific needs.

The lists are fairly comprehensive and as such look a little daunting. Go through them and decide where you need to take a shortcut or adapt the methodology to take account of your specific case and timescale constraints. Sometimes you have to go for it and leave a few stones unturned.

Reflect on each item and assess a current strategy project you are working on. Assess each activity using a simple RAG scale for status, where Red suggests major concerns and that immediate corrective actions are needed, Amber suggest some concerns and risks, and needs to be monitored closely, and Green indicates the activity is a priority and is on track.

WORKPLAN	DESCRIPTION OF POSSIBLE ACTIVITIES	STATUS
Stage 1 Start the process		
1 Project scope	Speak to your boss to identify the project scope and priorities	☐
2 Strategy team	Identify the key team members	☐
3 Strategic priorities	Review strategic, product–market and brand imperatives to identify strategy scope, direction and product/market/process priorities	☐
4 Strategy stakeholders	Identify the key stakeholders and meet with them individually	☐
5 Project plan	Put together a project plan for developing the strategic plan	☐
6 Resources	Ensure any necessary resources are available – e.g. budget, office facilities, etc.	☐
7 Technology	Ensure that the technology needed is in place and working. All team members should have access to the knowledge-sharing systems	☐
Stage 2 Take stock		
1 Market analysis	Conduct analysis to understand macro-economic trends, current and prospective customers, end users/consumers and key competitors. Research best practices and market leaders – create PESTEL analysis	☐
2 Internal audit	Conduct an internal audit of core capabilities (all aspects of the supply chain) and summarise in the form of critical strengths and weaknesses. Review the databases of internal lessons learned	☐
3 Idea generation workshop	Identify emerging opportunities and threats and collect initial ideas from primary and secondary sources. Use brainstorming techniques and other creative tools to generate ideas from the historical insights/lessons learned and analysis. This step is sometimes referred to as 'ideation'	☐

WORKPLAN	DESCRIPTION OF POSSIBLE ACTIVITIES	STATUS

Stage 2 Take stock (contd)

4	Customer reviews/ focus group responses	Gather current information from existing clients and potential clients either through focus group interviews or other market gathering. Analyse results for input to strategy review process	☐
5	Buying criteria	Create a buying criteria list with scores of client-desired features and achieved features – one table for each market segment (see Chapter 3, page 44.)	☐
6	SWOT	Create a SWOT matrix out of the first strategy workshop	☐

Stage 3 Review high-level themes

1	Mission statement	Create a mission statement if one does not exist (opportunity to modify existing statement)	☐
2	High-level target market statement	Create a high-level statement of market presence and products made – usually agreed at the first workshop	
3	Statement of competitive advantage	Draw up a statement of the competitive advantage that will underpin the strategic plan – to be agreed at first workshop	☐
4	Statement of beliefs	Develop a list of assumptions or 'beliefs' that the strategy will be based on. This may include statements about the market, competition or the organisation itself. Each needs to be backed up with evidence	☐
5	Organisational values	Develop or review the 'statement of values' that guides the company as to its culture and way of operating	☐

Stage 4 Agree high-level objectives

1	Vision statement	Create a vision statement that describes the future in motivational terms that the organisation is looking to achieve	☐
2	High-level corporate objectives	Develop a set of balanced high-level objectives that the organisation seeks to achieve. These objectives should be in the four quadrants of customer, process, people and finance, and they should be SMART (see Chapter 3, page 64)	

WORKPLAN	DESCRIPTION OF POSSIBLE ACTIVITIES	STATUS

Stage 5 Target key products and markets

1	Segmentation	Agree product and market segmentation for existing products	☐
2	New business development	Agree different new market, new product, new business and diversification opportunities. Discuss the relative advantages and disadvantages of each and finalise by creating the product–market matrix	☐
3	Product–market matrix	Create a product–market matrix showing emphasis in different areas (if appropriate)	☐
4	Review options	Review the proposed strategic end game in terms of products and markets. Align it to the high-level business objectives and verify that the solution chosen is the best solution to achieve these. It is possible to review both the strategy and even the objectives at this point	☐
5	Communicate to functional teams	Summarise the strategy process thus far in terms of the high-level objectives and high-level product marketing approach to achieve those objectives	☐
6	Corporate initiatives	Develop the corporate change programmes that will be needed to deliver the high-level strategic objectives	☐

Stage 6 Extend to develop internal capability and functional plans

1	Assign team	Ensure that the teams are assembled in each of the functional areas that need to support the business plan	☐
2	Functional-level objectives	Develop objectives for each functional unit, which tie back to the high-level objectives	☐
3	Functional plan	Develop the functional plan to meet the high-level and function-specific objectives. Create functional projects and identify budget and resources needed to support these as well as the corporate programmes	☐
4	Budget	Develop functional budgets for both operational expenditure and capital expenditure	☐
5	Resource plan	Develop a functional resource plan required to fulfil corporate objectives, including any organisational changes if required	☐
6	Functional project plan	Develop a high-level functional project plan showing key milestones and deliverables	☐

WORKPLAN	DESCRIPTION OF POSSIBLE ACTIVITIES	STATUS
Stage 7 Generate a risk register and future-proof the plan		
1 Risk register	Create a risk register and develop mitigation plans for the major risks	☐
2 Contingency planning	Look at different scenarios (positive and negative) and analyse the impact they would have on the successful execution of the strategy. Develop plans to prepare for the most likely scenarios	☐
Stage 8 Integrate all corporate-wide projects and key activities		
1 Project portfolio	Collect all of the projects, corporate programmes and major tasks that need to be completed into one database or table	☐
2 Project plan	Develop task-based (Gantt) and network-based (PERT) plans. Summarise the plan into one high-level network-style plan – using input from individual functional plans	☐
3 Risk register update	Update the risk register based on high-risk areas of multiple projects and programmes delivering against the same dates with shared or over-committed resources	☐
4 Budget	Develop an overall budget to achieve corporate objectives	☐
Stage 9 Engage and empower the organisation with good communication		
1 Strategic plan completion	Complete the overall organisational strategy document, combining deliverables from previous stages, including the strategic context, corporate objectives, programmes and budgets	☐
2 Stakeholder sign-off	Obtain sign-off from all stakeholders to the plan. Conduct formal close-down reviews (meetings) with key stakeholders, including user/customer/consumer groups and supply chain	☐
3 Communications plan	Develop a communications plan describing how the key messages will be presented to the different stakeholders and how ongoing communication should take place	☐
4 Communicate	Communicate to the organisation as per the communication plan to ensure everyone in the organisation knows their role in the strategy	☐
5 Media strategy	Complete a detailed media strategy (if required) with question and answers (Q&As), statements, press releases, etc.	☐
6 Team	Congratulate the team, update personal development congratulations plans (PDPs) and agree next roles	☐

WORKPLAN	DESCRIPTION OF POSSIBLE ACTIVITIES	STATUS
Stage 10 Supervise progress and governance		
1 Implementation	Kick off the new corporate initiatives as described in the strategy	☐
2 Governance schedule	Ensure regular strategy reviews are scheduled with appropriate senior managers	☐
3 Project portfolio review	Review the portfolio of strategic projects in terms of progress and continued relevance to the strategic priorities	☐
4 Risk register review	Review the risk register and monitor key risks	☐
5 Performance reviews	Set performance plans against corporate (and functional) objectives and for all employees and review them regularly	☐
6 Lessons learned	Capture and share learning and insights with other teams, update 'best practice' databases and communicate to interested parties	☐

THE FAST TRACK WAY

Take time to reflect

Within the Fast Track series, we cover a lot of ground quickly. Depending on your current role, company or situation, some ideas will be more relevant than others. Go back to your individual and team audits and reflect on the 'gaps' you have identified, and then take time to review each of the top ten tools and techniques and list of technologies.

Next steps

Based on this review, you will identify many ideas about how to improve your performance, but look before you leap: take time to plan your next steps carefully. Rushing into action is rarely the best way to progress unless you are facing a crisis. Think carefully about your own personal career development and that of your team. Identify a starting place and consider what would have a significant impact on performance and be easy to implement. Then make a simple to-do list with timings for completion.

Staying ahead

Finally, the fact that you have taken time to read and think hard about the ideas presented here suggests that you are already a professional in your chosen discipline. However, all areas of business leadership are changing rapidly and you need to take steps to stay ahead as a leader in your field. Take time to log in to the Fast Track web-resource, at **www.Fast-Track-Me.com**, and join a community of like-minded professionals.

Good luck!

OTHER TITLES IN THE FAST TRACK SERIES

This title is one of many in the Fast Track series that you may be interested in exploring. Whilst each title works as a standalone solution, together they provide a comprehensive cross-functional approach that creates a common business language and structure. The series includes title on the following:

→ Innovation

→ Project management

→ Finance

→ Sales

→ Marketing

GLOSSARY

7-S model This was an important model developed by Pascale and Athos. From their work with successful Japanese companies, they identified seven key levers available to management to deliver success – strategy, structure, systems, staff, style, skills and shared values. In their 7-S model, they noted that Japanese companies gave particular attention to the four 'soft' levers, namely staff, skills, style and shared values. To quote Takeo Fujisawa, co-founder of Honda Motor Company, 'Japanese and American management is 95 per cent the same and differs in all important respects'[1]

action plan The output from developing strategy, which lists the activities that need to be performed to achieve the strategic goals

adoption curve The phases through which consumers or the market as a whole move when adopting a new product or service: innovators, early adopters, early majority, late majority, laggards

alignment The process of ensuring that all the departmental or divisional strategies are consistent and supportive of the top-level strategy

analysis Formal evaluation of data or known facts in order to come to a conclusion. In the context of strategy, analysis looks at internal and external factors that currently influence, and may influence in the future, an organisation's strategy

Ansoff product–market growth matrix The Ansoff product–market growth matrix was created by Igor Ansoff in 1957. He drew a matrix with existing and new markets on one axis and existing and new products on the other. This gave four quadrants, with the strategic option for each cell shown in brackets.

1 Existing products in existing markets (market penetration).
2 Existing products in new markets (market development).
3 New products in existing markets (product development).
4 New products in new markets (diversification).

This representation allows you to summarise your current situation and evaluate different strategies for the future

awareness A measure of how many or what percentage of target customers are aware of a particular product or brand

balanced scorecard A group of performance indicators covering four categories:

1 financial results;
2 customer and brand;
3 operational excellence; and
4 people and learning

BCG growth–share matrix The BCG growth–share matrix was developed by Bruce Henderson of the Boston Consulting Group in the 1970s.[1] It consists of a Boston matrix with axes of market share relative to the largest competitor (x-axis) and financial growth rate (y-axis). This gives four types of business.

1 Cash cows – high market share, but low market growth.
2 Stars – high market share and high market growth.

---

[1]Stern, Carl W. and Deimler, Michael S. (2006 2nd edition), *The Boston Consulting Group on Strategy*, Hoboken, NJ: John Wiley & Sons.

3 Dogs – low market share and low growth.

4 Question marks – low market share and high growth.

This model is based on two main assumptions (which do not always hold true), namely:

→ an increase in market share will result in an increase in the generation of cash;

→ a growing market requires investment and therefore cash

benchmarking A method of comparing the performance of one company or process with others, including the market leader or best practice

benefit An attribute of a product or service expressed in terms of the positive impact it has on the user

best practice Processes, skills and systems that are considered to deliver optimum performance. These are often associated with market leaders

Boston matrix A business tool originally developed by the Boston Consulting Group. It is a chart with two values for the x-axis and two for the y-axis, giving four quadrants. An example is the BCG growth-share matrix

brainstorming A method of generating new ideas around a particular topic within a group situation. The key is to make the initial list quickly without discussion before evaluating the list as a whole

brand A name, design or feature that distinguishes one product or company from another. The brand is often associated with perceptions and perceived benefits

breakthrough A fundamentally different idea or way of thinking that is clearly distinctive when compared with similar ideas

business case A formal analysis of a new idea to validate whether it will provide a satisfactory return on the investment required to make it happen

business model A way of representing the key financial and operational parameters of an organisation, usually with the ability to vary one parameter and measure its impact on others

business to business (B2B) Commercial transactions between two organisations which do not involve sales directly to consumers

business to consumer (B2C) Commercial transactions between an organisation and the consumer which do not go through a third-party channel

cannibalisation The amount of demand for a new product that results from the erosion of demand for a current product or service. This has to be taken into consideration when calculating the real return on investment of a new idea

champion The person who is prepared to ensure that a new idea is implemented effectively. This person is often a senior manager with a high degree of passion or vested interest in the success of the new idea

commercialisation The process of taking a new product or service idea to a commercial market in order to gain profitable returns, typically involving sales, marketing and supply chain developments

competitive intelligence Information about competitors that enables an organisation to gain competitive advantage. For example, this may relate to their strengths and weaknesses, or their plans for new product introductions

competitor analysis The formal analysis of a competitor, involving the review of their financial performance, as well as their strategy, operations, product lines and customer base

consumer The user of a product or service. This may or may not be the person who buys it

contingency plan A plan to mitigate the effects of a potential problem, should it occur. This is particularly useful when introducing complex ideas or ideas that are critical to future business performance

core benefit proposition (CBP) The main benefit of value that customers will receive as a result of adopting a new idea

core competence The capabilities of an organisation that an organisation excels in and in which it typically has to maintain a high-level of capability to be competitive

corporate culture The values, operating principles or shared beliefs within an organisation. This is heavily influenced by the founders or the chief executive and will affect the adoption of a culture of continuous innovation

creativity The process of thinking about and generating new ideas

critical assumption An assumption made about the future that will have a significant impact on the success or failure of a new idea. Each assumption will have associated risks that should be mitigated

critical success factors (CSF) Factors of a new idea or its implementation that are necessary for successful introduction

culture The style and values of an organisation and the working behaviours that employees exhibit as a consequence

customer The person who purchases a product or service

customer needs Specific problems to be solved by a customer

customer value analysis A structured approach to analysis of customer musts and wants, showing how a company performs against its competitors

dashboard An electronic (computer) display of information relating to the performance of a team, process, product or business

decision tree A process for making decisions where ideas (or choices) and alternative outcomes are presented in the form of branches on a tree

differentiation The distinct attributes or features of an idea that help to provide a source of advantage over competitors

directional policy matrix (or GE-McKinsey matrix) The directional policy matrix (or GE-McKinsey matrix) built on the BCG growth–share matrix to provide a more representative analysis of the business. It charts 'relative competitive strength' as the (horizontal) x-axis and 'relative segment attractiveness' as the (vertical) y-axis. Each market segment is shown as a circle – the diameter of the circle is proportional to the revenue from that segment, and a solid slice of each 'pie' represents the market share. Companies should invest in the 'top right' opportunities, i.e. where the market is attractive and the competitive position good. Companies at the opposite end, with low opportunity and low market share, should be divested. For those in between, the company has to make a strategic choice – to invest with a view to increasing market share, to manage for cash, or to divest

disruptive strategy The creation and launch of a completely new product, service or process improvement idea as opposed to incremental change. It often results from the adoption of a new technology or major market trend

early adopters Customers who will use their own judgement to adopt a new product or service very early on in its life cycle

economic value add (EVA) The financial value associated with a new idea, taking into account life cycle costs and benefits entrepreneur A person who initiates, leads, takes the risks and gets the rewards from a new venture

exit strategy A plan for withdrawing a new idea at a point in time. This might be due to a limited market or declining performance. This term also refers to a planned sale of a business by its founders

experience curve The experience curve effect states that as people or organisations gain more experience in performing a task, they also become more efficient at it. This is one of the assumptions of the BCG growth–share matrix

features Characteristics of an idea, product or service that provide benefits to customers or consumers

first to market The first product or service in a new emerging market. These products will often gain what is called first mover or prime mover advantage

five forces See *Porter's five forces*

focus group A market research method where a group of customers meets in one room to discuss the pros and cons associated with an idea

Gantt chart A plan of activities within a project presented graphically as a series of boxes against a timeline. This technique was developed by Henry Gantt as a highly effective way of communicating project plans and progress to stakeholders

gap analysis An assessment of the difference between the current performance and the desired or target performance

innovation The commercial exploitation of ideas. Creativity relates to the generation of ideas, whereas the strategy process embraces implementation of those ideas within the market or business context

insight New information that is of potential value to the recipient or their team/organisation

intellectual property (IP) Information relating to an idea, including proprietary knowledge, designs and brands, that is formally protected by law

intrapreneur Someone who develops new enterprises within a much larger organisation. Similar to entrepreneur, but working for someone else

kaizen A Japanese term meaning continuous improvement

learning organisation An organisation or team that adopts a structured approach to the capture and sharing of insights of lessons learned from operational activities such as the introduction of new products

life-cycle cost The total cost of implementing a new idea from concept and implementation to operational status and ongoing support

market development Activities to take an existing product or service into a new market or to grow the overall size and shape of the market

market research Analysis of a market in order to understand its various attributes in terms of size and growth, segmentation, customer decision criteria and competition

market share Sales of a particular product, service or firm as a percentage of the overall market

market testing The formal evaluation of a new idea with customers, either within a controlled environment, such as a focus group, or within a pilot market

marketing Activities to increase the awareness of a new idea, product or service within a target customer group

markets A collection of current or potential customers

maturity The stage of the product life cycle where there are only a few remaining prospective customers. These customers are often the most difficult ones to convince and the market is often very competitive

metrics Key performance indicators used to assess the value of a new idea. These should ideally be balanced in terms of financial, operational and strategic indicators

nemawashi A Japanese term meaning to 'nurture the roots' of an idea. Many ideas stand a better chance of being supported by others if the 'seeds' of the idea are planted in meetings and discussions before any formal decision point

net present value (NPV) A method of calculating the value of a new idea at a point in the future. It takes projected future cash flows (profits) discounted by the level of risk associated with each period. Typically the more risky an idea, the less certainty there will be with future forecasts and the lower the NPV

new product development (NPD) The process for developing a new product from initial concept or idea to in-market commercialisation

offensive strategy The development of new ideas in order to exploit an opportunity in the market or to aggressively attack a competitor

opportunity cost The lost benefits of indirect costs associated with the adoption of an idea. For example, developing one product may prohibit the development of an alternative product

Pareto profile A graphical representation of a series of ideas, products or markets, ordered to show those with the highest value or contribution at one end, descending to the lowest contribution. This technique is useful for getting a team to identify and focus on priorities

patent The legal protection of an idea that protects the concept or design from being copied or reverse-engineered by competitors for a period of time

perceived use value (PUV) A technique for identifying the value the customer gets from different features of a product. This may not necessarily be proportional to the cost of providing the feature

performance indicators Measures of performance associated with an idea. They should be SMART: specific to the idea, measurable, achievable, realistic and time-bound

pipeline A list of future ideas for consideration or implementation

Porter's five forces An analytical framework developed by Michael Porter to analyse the current trends and drivers in an industry. Opportunities will be identified wherever there is a significant change or 'discontinuity' in the industry. Although there are many pressures on a business, Porter identified five in particular that have a direct effect for each organisation. These five forces are:

1 the direct competitors (the fewer the better);
2 new entrants (the more difficult for them to set up and compete the better);
3 substitute products – different products which compete for the same spend (the fewer the better);
4 suppliers (the more the merrier);
5 customers (the more the merrier)

portfolio A group of ideas, projects, products or markets(see also *project portfolio*)

portfolio map A graphical representation of a portfolio of ideas or projects, used to identify the relative strengths and weaknesses of each item. Axes will vary but most common will be market attractiveness and competitive position

price elasticity A way of assessing how sensitive customers are to changes in the pricing of a product. If a product is 'elastic', it means customers are sensitive to price changes; 'inelastic' means customers are not sensitive to price change

process champion The person responsible for the design, management and continuous improvement of an operational process. Process strategy is necessary in order to improve overall effectiveness and efficiency

process map A graphical representation of a process, where the activities are linked to show the natural sequence and are displayed against roles (known as a 'swim lane format'). Process maps are useful analytic tools for identifying opportunities for process improvement

process re-engineering A structured approach to the fundamental redesign of a process, often starting with a blank piece of paper

products Goods or services created and sold to customers

product development The process for developing a new product or service from initial concept or idea to in-market commercialisation

product life cycle The stages that a new product will go through: introduction, growth, maturity and decline

product line A group of products or services with similar characteristics or attributes, possibly sold under the same brand

project A series of activities designed to deliver a goal, with an agreed start and end point

project portfolio A group of ideas or projects. If they are related or have a common shared goal they would be referred to as a programme

protection A means of ensuring that the new idea is not immediately stolen and used by competitors. This can sometimes be achieved through legal protection such as patents and trademarks

prototype A model of the final solution that can be tested in order to de-risk the final idea

qualitative market research A structured approach to conducting market research, working with consumers (individually or in groups) to ascertain their needs. This helps those in the marketing and product development teams understand why consumers buy certain products and services

quality assurance/compliance The function in a business responsible for monitoring processes to ensure they comply with agreed standards

quality function deployment (QFD) A structured approach for linking the needs of the market (musts and wants) with the development of a new idea (features/attributes)

quantitative market research Consumer research conducted through surveys in order to identify needs for different groups or segments in the market. In order for the results to be valid, the group size needs to be large and representative of the larger population

resource matrix A two-dimensional grid that shows which people (or other resources such as facilities, equipment, material and budgets) will be required on which projects and when

responsibility matrix A two-dimensional grid that shows which members of a project team are involved in which activities

return on investment (ROI) A standard measure of the financial rewards associated with a project as a ratio of the investment required to make it happen

risk A potential problem associated with a new idea that could occur in the future. Each risk should be identified and quantified as the combination of the probability of it happening (P) and the impact if it were to happen (I). Agreement is then needed on the mitigating actions – who does what, when?

risk management The process of mitigating the impact of identified risks. Actions will be preventive (proactive action taken to prevent the risk occurring) or contingent (reactive action taken to minimise the impact if it does occur)

roadmapping A graphical representation of future intentions to introduce new ideas, technology or projects

Sarbanes-Oxley The Sarbanes-Oxley Act of 2002, also called SOx or Sarbox, is a US federal law enacted on 30 July 2002 to improve corporate accountability in response to a number of major corporate and accounting scandals

satisfaction surveys A structured process for capturing feedback from customers in order to identify their overall level of satisfaction with the product or service that has been provided. Unfortunately, these surveys are often not a good predictor of future intentions to purchase

scanning A systematic approach to analyse the industry and market in order to identify opportunities for new ideas. The results should feed into forums for strategy and review

scenario planning A process of identifying and evaluating alternative future states. Future scenarios are identified by looking at future trends or possible outcomes in the market

search and development (S&D) A phrase reflecting the fact that much strategy comes from searching the internet for good ideas, learning from others and then replicating or replacing rather than starting from scratch

segmentation The process of dividing a large market into smaller groups. Each sub-group will have similar characteristics and will therefore simplify the process of analysis and targeting

sensitivity analysis An assessment of the impact of changing a single variable on the overall performance or result

stage-gate process A structured process used to develop and commercialise new ideas. Each stage will have clear outputs or deliverables. A Go/No Go decision will typically be made at the end of each stage gate or phase

strategy The future vision and the plan of how to get there: the basis on which an organisation or team will compete or differentiate itself, its products and services and its target markets and customers

strategic canvas A way of showing the relative importance of different product attributes by drawing them on a chart. The idea was published by Kim and Mauborgne in 2002[2]

strategic partnering An alliance or partnership between two organisations to improve their operational processes, create new products or exploit new markets

strategy review board A group of managers and subject matter experts that reviews the organisation's strategy on a regular basis to ensure it remains relevant and competitive

substitute Where an alternative product is available to meet a customer need but which is not a direct competitor – an example might be a restaurant competing with a cinema. They offer different services but compete for the same entertainment cash

suggestion scheme A process by which new ideas identified by employees are captured, sorted and fed into a forum for future evaluation. This process is increasingly managed through websites

[2]Kim, W. Chan and Mauborgne, Renée (2002), 'Charting your company's future', *Harvard Business Review*, June.

supply chain A group of companies involved in the supply of products and services to consumers, where each company will be a supplier to one of the others

SWOT analysis An assessment of an idea, product or market using four criteria: strengths, weaknesses, opportunities and threats. It can also be used to summarise environmental criteria

target market The group of customers or consumers that is most likely to buy the product or that represents the most significant strategic potential

technology roadmap A top-level plan or graphic that shows how technology will evolve over future periods and how it will impact the evolution of products and processes

technology transfer The process of transferring expertise, knowledge and intellectual property (IP) from one organisation to another

test market A market of limited scope used to test a new idea. It needs to be small enough to mitigate the risk of failure, but it also needs to reflect the target market so that results will guide implementation

think tank A group or environment set up specifically to generate and evaluate new ideas. It will often be very distinct from typical operations in order to identify more creative and distinctive solutions

thinking hats A term developed by Edwards de Bono to reflect the differing roles that people can fulfil during a meeting or workshop. This approach can be a stimulus for creative thinking

time to market The time taken to develop a new idea from concept to implementation or initial sales in the market. For some organisations, a faster time to market will provide a source of advantage

total quality management (TQM) A methodology and associated toolset used for the continuous improvement of a team or process

trademarks Registered brands or logos that prohibit others from copying or mimicking the design

unique selling proposition (USP) A distinctive set of features and benefits that deliver a competitive advantage in the market. The USP can only be identified through a detailed understanding of customer wants and needs and of competitor performance

user Any person who uses a product or a service. As the consumer, they will gain the benefit but they will not necessarily be the buyer

value added The result of adding or combining features to a product or service in order to increase the overall worth

value chain/value chain analysis Popularised by Michael Porter,[3] this is the idea that as a product moves through each stage of its development from idea to implementation, value is added. The value chain identifies each step and relative value added. Value-adding activities can either be primary activities (e.g. logistics, manufacturing, sales and service) or support activities (e.g. IT, HR and procurement). The value added and costs incurred are assessed for each step in the value chain. The strategic goal is then to maximise the value added and minimise the costs for each stage. The value chain concept can also be extended beyond individual organisations and be applied to whole supply chains and distribution networks

[3]Porter, Michael E. (1998), *Competitive Advantage: Creating and Sustaining Superior Performance*, New York: Simon & Schuster.

value proposition A simple statement that describes the value a product or service gives to the customer or consumer. The word 'value' implies that it will describe benefits (possibly measured in financial terms) and not features or attributes

virtual team A team working towards a common purpose but not located in the same facility. Through the use of technology, this team may not come together at all

vision A view of the future state of the business: what it could be if everything went according to plan. Visions tend to talk about a point in the future in general and inspirational terms

voice of the customer (VOC) An understanding of the musts and wants of different customer or consumer groups and the relevance to the organisation and individual teams

VRIO A tool for analysing businesses. It is an acronym for four questions that determine the competitive potential of a resource or capability.

It is important to meet these criteria to maintain competitive advantage.

1 Value – is there an opportunity to exploit this capability to deliver value (profit) for the organisation?
2 Rarity – is this capability or resource scarce (and likely to have a higher value)?
3 Imitability – is this capability or resource difficult (e.g. expensive or technically complex) to copy so that its advantages will endure?
4 Organisation – is the company well enough organised to take advantage of this resource or capability?

whiteboard A board for capturing ideas, secured to the wall of a corridor or work room in order to allow ideas for performance improvement to be captured

window of opportunity The period of time during which a new idea or product can be launched successfully

INDEX

Page numbers in **bold** relate to entries in the Glossary.

FAST TRACK TO SUCCESS

9780273719908

9780273721789

9780273721802

9780273719885

9780273719922

9780273721765

EVERYTHING YOU NEED TO ACCELERATE YOUR CAREER

FT Prentice Hall
FINANCIAL TIMES